Grouse and Gun

Grouse and Gun

G. L. CARLISLE

STANLEY PAUL
London Melbourne Auckland Johannesburg

Stanley Paul & Co. Ltd

An imprint of Century Hutchinson Ltd

Brookmount House, 62–65 Chandos Place, Covent Garden,
London WC2N 4NW

Century Hutchinson Australia (Pty) Ltd
PO Box 496, 16–22 Church Street, Hawthorn, Victoria 3122

Century Hutchinson New Zealand Limited
32–34 View Road, PO Box 40–086, Glenfield, Auckland 10

Century Hutchinson South Africa (Pty) Ltd
PO Box 337, Bergvlei 2012, South Africa

First published 1983
Reprinted 1987
Copyright © G. L. Carlisle 1983

Set in Linotron Bembo by Rowland Phototypesetting Ltd
Bury St Edmunds, Suffolk

Printed in Great Britain by
Redwood Burn Limited, Trowbridge, Wiltshire
and bound by Anchor Brendon Ltd,
Tiptree, Essex

British Library Cataloguing in Publication Data

Carlisle, G. L.
    Grouse and gun.
    1. Grouse shooting
    I. Title
    799.2'48616   SK325.G7

ISBN 0 09 153360 0

Contents

List of Illustrations

Photographs

Line Drawings

Foreword

As I sat on my shooting stick peering over the top of a grouse butt, I could just make out the line of beaters about a mile and a half away, starting the drive and coming down from the hill that lay in front. It wasn't a very steep hill, just a gradual incline rising gently to the horizon. I could see the white flags begin to show as the beaters moved off and the drive began.

It was a beautiful September morning with a brisk south-west wind. The colours of the moor were shades of purple, brown, green and yellow and I felt exhilarated to be in such a place. The beaters on the left seemed to hold back whilst the right hand members of the team moved forward slowly and steadily across the moor; no doubt they were allowing for the wind. Suddenly, what looked to me like a dark shadow about a mile away moved across the moor from my right to left; a pretty good pack of grouse was on the move, about fifty or so, I estimated. Then the pack disappeared into a fold in the ground. The right hand beaters must have turned them because back they came again, only this time there were many, many more and as they flew steadily on about half a mile away, diagonally towards the butts, other grouse set flight from the heather to swell their numbers.

Will the flankers catch them up and turn them? Yes, here they come, Great Scot, what a sight! They will miss number 1 butt, however I am in number 3 so will get a chance. Number 2 butt opens up; now it's my turn; the air is full of grouse, some in front of the butts, some behind, swerving and jinking as the pack goes relentlessly on down the line. The drive continued, with more grouse coming in packs, coveys, pairs and singles. And the later drives were nearly as good.

As I drove home I thought about this wonderful day. There had been much discussion about the numbers of grouse in the big pack during the first drive; some said there must have been between five and eight hundred. I turned my thoughts to the birds themselves, and what wonderful all rounders they are. They live in beautiful surroundings, are attractive to look at, extremely sporting to shoot, excellent foreign currency earners and, what is more, very good to eat!

In this book Gordon Carlisle has gathered together much of the knowledge of the old authors, together with some practical and interesting information on the present day situation. The results of his research and detailed observation will appeal to everyone concerned with grouse, and not only the shooting of them.

Biddulph

Preface

This is a book about grouse, and how they live, and the great variety of people who are concerned in their conservation, and about the sport of shooting.

In case it may seem presumptuous to be writing on such a wide subject I must at once acknowledge my debt to the authors of the books listed in Appendix C. Much of their wisdom and experience is distilled here, and sometimes quoted.

Not being within a million miles of owning or even leasing any shooting myself I have tried to avoid the parochial outlook of some of the authors; they often have *very* firm views of what they did on their moors, without bothering too much about how others may operate in quite different circumstances, even in a different country.

The object of the book is certainly not to teach owners or tenants how to run their shoots, but rather to explain to their guests and customers what a lot there is to be done and worried about all through the year.

I hope newcomers to grouse shooting will learn something of the preliminaries to their day, and of the less obvious happenings during it. Possibly some may prefer not to, believing with Erich Maria Remarque: 'Never lose your ignorance; you cannot replace it.' That, even more so, could apply to those opposed to shooting who may nevertheless learn something here, if they have a mind to.

It seems that less books are written about grouse now than used to be the case. The old ones often contain some marvellously high-flown ideas of how things ought to be, perhaps were. Like this: grouse shooters from the south should 'help the dwellers of the far north to share the hard-earned gold of England's wealthier citizens'!

And a pleasantly modern-sounding comment on the lack of exactitude by the Press, who displayed 'an ignorance of the subject that was remarkable even among journalistic contributions to sporting literature'.

Much late Victorian literature was effusive and sentimental: the birds of the morning heard by a visitor to the moor are described as 'feathered songsters vying with each other to excel in praise of the God that made them'!

But, after all, they had many different ideas in those days: Highland keepers had a profitable sideline in catching fox cubs, sometimes in rubber-jawed traps, and sending them south to the English hunts.

My thanks are due to all those kind people listed in Appendix G. They provided help and information and practical demonstration. Especially I must thank Priscilla, my wife, for inspiration, for taking some of the photographs and for accompanying me on our happy visits to so many grouse occasions.

1 *The Moor*

The car driving along the moorland road stops; the driver gets out, leans on the roof and then points across the heather, indicating something to his family.

In the middle distance, behind a line of butts, men stand in anticipation. All is quiet, warm, soporific on this fine August day. Nearby is a faintly tinkling stream, and scudding cloud shadows cross the purple, green and grey landscape. A blue hare lollops close to the nearest butt; nobody pays any attention. Sheep approach, winding like an undulating white caterpillar along a track. Beyond the butts on the brow of a distant hill several deer appear; they gaze momentarily at the scene and then pick their way unhurriedly over the ridge.

Suddenly a gun cracks twice; the first covey of birds has flicked past the furthest butt, low and almost unobserved. The watchers by the car see another covey, higher and visible against the sky; it drops into the heather 50 yards in front of the butts. And then many birds come streaming over, swinging across the line and swerving in all directions. Puffs of smoke appear and all the guns crash into action. Away over to the right can be seen the spaced-out line of beaters appearing and disappearing in the folds of the ground, and swinging their flags from side to side.

'Is that grouse shooting, Dad, like you used to do?' asks one of the boys in the car.

'Yes, but there's a lot more to it than that.'

The origin of the name 'grouse' is probably an old French word 'griesche' which signified grey or speckled. The bird used to be called moor-fowl, moor-game, and sometimes moor-cock, gorcock, moor-henne and heather-hen, but the French word became modified to 'grows' in an ordinance of Henry VIII's in 1531; and although this really applied to the blackcock, whose mate is not so dissimilar to the grouse, the term came to be used more or less exclusively for the red grouse.

The first recorded instance of grouse driving seems to have been at Cannon Hall, Barnsley, Yorkshire; in 1805 the keeper, George Fisher, drove the moor for the benefit of the sons of the owner, Mr Spencer Stanhope, the boys hiding among the rocks. Thirty years later drives had become a regular feature of the shooting, using holes dug in the ground as butts, an idea that started when a certain sandhole used for road repair material became a favourite place to conceal a Gun. By 1843 a bag of fifty brace a day had been achieved and local newspapers were referring to 'the unsportsmanlike practice of driving grouse'.

Other moor owners began to adopt the driving technique, building above-ground butts known as 'batteries'. By the 1860s and 1870s very big bags were being taken at such famous names as High Force, Broomhead, Studley Royal, Wemmergill, Raby and Bolton Abbey in the counties of Northumberland, Durham and Yorkshire. The change to driving was one of the main reasons for the increased stock of birds and the subsequent bags, because it reduced the numbers of old birds. These bellicose old ones always grab large territories and chase away younger, fitter and more fecund birds which, left to themselves, would breed bigger coveys on smaller areas of ground. In the old ways of shooting by walking-up or dogging, the older birds usually rose first and escaped while their following young were shot. The old birds, however, also rose first when they were driven, and then they reached the butts first and were more likely to be shot. Again, the large packs of wild birds which formed later in the season could not be approached by dogs, but could be driven over concealed shooters.

Butts built on the side of a hill, by digging out some of the earth and piling it up on the downhill side, become partly sunken rather than standing up their full height from ground level. This type was known as a 'Liggin hoile', in the Yorkshire dialect, describing a hole that you could lie in.

An interesting sidelight of the proliferation of driving in England was that the size of the bags in the late nineteenth century far outclassed those of Scotland, hitherto regarded as the superior grouse-producing area. The National Shooting Survey programme, however, set up by the British Association for Shooting and Conservation in 1979 to discover the geo-graphical distribution of the bag of various game species in the UK, showed that the numbers of grouse shot in Scotland and England were very nearly equal. Alas, Scotland now lags behind.

The red grouse *(Lagopus lagopus scoticus)* is the only British bird which is not found in any other country. Its habitat is decided chiefly by the presence of its main food, heather, and it thrives in the climate of high ground. The bird therefore frequents the open moorland of Scotland, including the Orkneys and Hebrides, northern England down to Yorkshire and Derbyshire, and north Wales, with a small number in Ireland. The appearance of the countryside in these different locations varies considerably.

Any moor at its best is a most lovely place. When the clouds are high, the sky blue and the heather still in fullest flower you cannot help rejoicing in the shapes and colours around you. In late August the bracken has not yet turned to russet, but here and there some strands have stolen a march on their fellows and changed to gold. Along the gulleys there are lumps and hum-mocks, hollows and drains, thick grass on the bank top, and reeds and a little stream along the bottom; dark boulders, light grey lichen-covered rocks and jet-black peat. In some eye-catching damp places lies the brightest emerald moss you ever saw.

As you stand knee deep in the purple heather you notice that nearby is much shorter heather, while beyond is a blackened burnt area dotted with the bleached skeletons of tough old heather plants. In the distance you can see a kind of chequerboard of these burnt patches, and perhaps you wonder if the fires have been started deliberately, and then controlled.

The moors in England often seem desolate, with miles of featureless green expanses, dry-stone walls, a few sheep and not much colour in the heather. Drive across Durham from Alston to Bishop Auckland, or across Yorkshire from Kirkby Stephen to Ripon and you may be disappointed at the lack of colour, but you will have been close to some first class grouse country. Somehow the Scottish moors, especially to a visiting southerner, usually look more dramatic and challenging, even inspiring.

The moors on the flanks of the Pennine chain tend to be flatter than those in Scotland; there is less heather except on the steeper parts, more grass and more sheep continuously grazing. But the underlying rock often contains much limestone which makes a fertile soil able to support plant life.

The richness of the soil affects its feeding potential for animals and birds and is a major factor towards making a good grouse moor; unfortunately, the latter can still be sufficiently mismanaged to produce far less birds than it should.

In the eighteenth century much of Scotland and the north of England was covered by forests. When these were cleared sheep were grazed over enormous areas; they formed the main economic product of the land. Grouse were shot almost entirely by the locals rather than by visiting sportsmen.

The sheep ate the grass and the heather, particularly the young heather, and the graziers were required to burn some of the old heather every year to encourage new growth. This they did, somewhat indiscriminately.

By the middle of the nineteenth century railways had simplified travel, even to Scotland, and the introduction of the breechloader was beginning to revolutionize game shooting. Before long landowners realized that they could get more rent from grouse shooters than from sheep farmers.

The shooters liked to see plenty of long heather, because they could approach closer to the birds, and so they stopped the shepherds burning it. Eventually there was almost no young heather left and the sheep's food supply dwindled. So some moors were burned again, for the sheep, and the owners of the shooting rights noticed that in those areas the numbers of grouse, which had been dwindling, picked up again. Heather burning then became universally practised once more, though it never caught up with the requirement of ensuring the supply of sufficient new growth each year; on nearly every moor it has

Heather burn pattern Several strips go up to the road, a natural fire break

A line of grouse butts with birds flying towards them. It is near the end of a drive and beaters can be seen approaching on the left

still failed to achieve this. (The subject is dealt with more fully in Chapter 4.)

Like any cultivated land, the moor requires mowing, pruning and weeding, although not fertilizing. Mowing and pruning is in fact done mostly by fire, although actual cutting can also be done. A machine towed by a tractor can operate in any direction and in wet weather; but many parts of the moor are inaccessible to a tractor. Burning is dependent on the wind, requires reasonably dry conditions and has a legal 'season' – you may not burn out of season because of the danger to wildlife.

Weeding consists of removing vegetation of no food value to bird or beast and harmful to good growth. The chief enemy here is bracken.

When you remember a green hillside where you walked as a child, do you not instantly recall the tall fronds of bracken? They made cunning places to hide in, and crawl through, and had that unpleasant way of cutting your fingers if you tried to pluck them. There is more of it now, increasing all the time and encroaching on upland areas; nearly all moors have too much, even up to around 1500 feet.

Bracken may enhance the beauty of the moor, with its pale green in spring, darker tone in summer and russet in autumn, but it is a menace.

It grows fast and kills the vegetation beneath it, including grass and heather. It can have poisonous effects if eaten by horses, pigs and cattle, and old dead bracken forms a thick mat of rotting rubbish which harbours ticks. These attack sheep and grouse, with deadly effect.

The old method of controlling bracken was to scythe it in early summer. Mechanical cutters and slashing machines can now be used and also rollers, but, as with heather cutting, often the steepness of the slopes and the many boulders make this impossible. The answer, although expensive, is to spray from a helicopter. May and Baker have a chemical called Asulox which has proved partially effective. (More details are given in Chapter 4.)

As regards fertilizing the moor, the specific advice from the Game Conservancy is *not* to do so. A nitrogenous fertilizer applied in spring will make the heather grow but this will attract deer, sheep and cattle; the extra grazing and the trampling effect is more likely to drive grouse away than increase the stock. Fertilizing is expensive, any beneficial effects are only short term, and the money and effort would be better spent on other ways of moor management.

Two features of a grouse moor which help to distinguish it from a truly wild stretch of countryside are roads and drains. In more leisurely days, when the shooting party walked or rode ponies, roads were less important; now, with the demand for swift transport to all parts of the moor, roads are needed and become one of the main expenses when opening up a moor for sport.

A small team with a mechanical digger may spend three months on a new, gravel road. First they scrape off the peat, then they hack out the rock and crush it small enough to be rolled in to make a good foundation. The type and hardness of the rock will greatly affect time and expense at this stage. It may be that small stone for the top surface can be obtained from a nearby quarry on the estate, which will help to keep down costs.

The road is best left for a year and then checked to see where it has settled and where the water lies. All along its course it will have ditches at the sides to drain off the rain, and frequently it will require a bridge; this may be a simple affair of a 2-foot-diameter iron pipe covered with rocks or it can involve beams and planks across a 20-foot gulley. All cost money and time.

When possible the team digs the road along the contours, to simplify drainage; in steep places hairpin bends will be required to keep the gradient reasonably shallow. The contractor stops work before the shooting season; if he started work in early May he will have completed perhaps 2 miles of road. The cost of opening up a neglected moor in this way may well be £30,000, or even twice that, but the owner will come to regard it as one of his best investments.

As with so many operations concerning the land, an agricultural grant may be obtainable: not to make a road so that idle grouse shooters do not have to walk, but to provide access to remote areas to enable the shepherd to reach his flock easily and quickly.

The moor also needs draining for it is quite surprisingly wet.

At 2000 feet or more you may find boggy places often beloved of red deer stags, who roll in the wet peat and come out looking fiercely black. The moor has many springs; these give birth to tumbling, gurgling streams which in winter become torrents. But in many places the ground remains a damp stagnant bog, useless for growing heather and entirely unattractive to grouse. And so furrows must be dug, usually by a special tractor-drawn plough, diagonally down the hill and leading towards a natural stream; these drain channels are often known as 'grips'. An added advantage of good draining is that the strongyle worm, purveyor of 'grouse disease' (see Chapter 2), is dependent on damp conditions for its existence. On well-drained ground, where the droppings of the host bird dry quickly, the worm dies.

Another sign of a grouse moor is the presence of beehives, first stages in the production of heather honey. Is any other more deliciously flavoured? Any expanse of heather can support bees, but the likelihood is that where the ground is looked after and cherished the quality of the heather will be far higher. So the chances are that your grouse moor will have settings of bee-hives, near the keeper's cottage, alongside the approach road and sometimes up one of those new roads towards the shooting area. You may wonder who owns the bees, and what he pays for the privilege of placing his hives in such profitably salubrious surroundings. Usually the owner is a local bee fancier, who obtains permission from the keeper in return for a few jars of honey at the end of the season.

What else does a grouse moor have? Well, of course, those lines of butts. You can shoot grouse without standing in a butt, but it is the regularly spaced little miniature forts, as seen from the road, that indicate where someone is looking after the land and enjoying the sport it can provide.

Butt building, and repair, is one of the gamekeeper's summer jobs. He uses natural materials whenever possible; sometimes when suitable stones are available the results are in the best tradition of skilful dry-stone-walling. A big circular butt, with a narrow entrance at one side and topped with turf, looks like a hut waiting to be roofed, almost good enough to live in. This type of butt is designed for return drives, that is, the occupying shooter can face either way according to how the grouse are being driven.

The upright screen type of butt is sometimes made of cut turf, or of wooden slats, or wood laced with heather; it can even be of dull-painted corrugated iron sheets. However made, the screen must be firmly secured otherwise it will be blown flat, or knocked down by cattle or sheep scratching themselves against it and climbing over it. The damage these animals can do has to be seen to be believed. Sometimes a protective fence of chestnut paling is needed to keep them away. The shooter can stand on either side of these rather skimpy and probably temporary screens.

Butts may, however, be required to face only one way, which makes floor construction and draining easier: the occupants must have a firm platform to stand on and a one-way butt needs this on one side only.

Sunken butts can be used on a hillside, when the drainage problem is easily solved. They have the advantage of a lower profile and thus being less conspicuous to approaching birds, but they are impracticable on flat, damp ground. Particularly unacceptable are plain screen butts or tumbledown stone butts, about 3 feet high, behind which a 6-foot man is expected to crouch!

The number of butts in a line should be more than the number of Guns expected to occupy them. Eight or nine Guns is the usual number and with ten or twelve butts available the decision on which end of the line to occupy, and which to leave blank, can be taken according to the weather conditions of the day.

The distance between butts should be 40 yards unless exceptional circumstances of ground dictate otherwise. If they are further apart birds flying between butts are not in range until they are very nearly in the danger zone where shooting is unsafe. When the occupants of two adjoining butts are out of sight of each other a post is erected between them as an indication of where the other fellow is.

The good solid stone-built butts are virtually permanent. They will be there, or perhaps they already have been, for a hundred years. Somebody must have thought carefully about their siting; what influenced him?

Circular butt Note guns in sleeves with carrying straps and leather cartridge bag. Top left is the distant lunch hut

A well-made butt on high ground with a good flat floor and natural drainage into a little water course. Stones are topped with turf and heather, butt faces only one way and is square – no doubt about which is the front

Wooden slat butt probably temporary, in an experimental position. It is square to the front and faces one way only. The birds are approaching nicely and there is plenty of room in the butt

A low-ground butt on swampy land where it is almost impossible to dig down far. The butt could have been built up higher with turves

Certain fairly well-defined flight lines occur on all moors, with variations according to the wind. These become familiar to the owner and his keeper, who site their butts accordingly. Temporary butts of the wooden-screen variety are used when trying out a new plan to find the best positions for intercepting the grouse. Thus the location of butts is determined by tradition and experience. When birds are driven along the side of a hill the butts are best sited where the hill is steepest, and the higher up the better: grouse usually fly along contour lines with a tendency to go higher, seldom lower.

But if the drive is across undulating ground, should the line of butts be along a crest or on the reverse slope beyond? The experts, backed by knowledge gained on their own hills, are apt to disagree. One says, 'Reverse slope is no good. Birds will settle on the crest just before they reach the Guns.' Another decrees, 'Butts on the skyline will turn the birds before they get in range.'

The wise shoot owner or manager permits himself a certain amount of experiment in determining butt positions, varying his drives occasionally and studying always the behaviour of the birds. Building, draining, maintaining and protecting butts is expensive; they also need inspecting, since all but the most sturdy are liable to damage by trespassers, some of whom have been known to treat a butt as a latrine.

This grouse moor, then, becomes recognizable as something more than just a heathery hill up there in the windy places. There is the pattern of the burned heather patches, a distinctly recognizable chequer-board of black and grey amongst the purple and the green. And the roads, light brown gravel ribbons, often with dark peat ditches at the side, curving across the slopes, mounting ever higher till they cross the distant horizon.

You can see the draining patterns, too, slanting across and often leading to a natural stream. The line of butts catches the eye, especially if it is close to the road. And there is a little black hut or bothy, perhaps two, out towards the middle of the area, you can see them from the footpath, where the shooting parties have their lunch.

The moor is a beautiful place, with many different moods, and supports an astonishing variety of wildlife. But not quite everything in this garden is lovely: bugs and disease lurk unseen and bad weather threatens.

Furthermore it is by no means certain that this grouse moor will exist as it is now for all that much longer. It may be ploughed up and planted with trees: softwood conifers, probably, because the financial return is quicker and because they are better suited to the higher ground and colder climate than hardwoods. Economic conditions have already persuaded some landowners that there is more profit and less trouble in forestry than in running a grouse shoot. Sad, like the farms where the turnover from letting caravan sites is higher than growing a crop of wheat.

The demand for paper, especially newsprint, increases steadily and this country imports by far the greater part of its requirements of timber. It would indeed be an ironic twist of circumstance if the moors did revert to trees again. Shooting, however, is likely to continue as long as a reasonable reconciliation of interests is achieved with the hill farmers, and the tourists who like walking and watching wildlife; also, tree growing becomes less economic the further up the mountain you go.

If it was not for the grouse the appearance of some 10 million acres of Scotland and the north of England would change drastically. Heather would deteriorate, the birds would become infinitely rarer and the ground would be covered by scrubby woodland, rank grasses and peat bogs. The magnificent beauty of the moors is very much dependent on their *management* and the preservation of the right habitat for grouse.

2 *The Birds*

Several varieties of grouse exist, in many different places. In the
northern hemisphere there are:

Black	Pinnated	Ruffed
Blue	Rock Ptarmigan	Sage
Red	White-tailed Ptarmigan	Sharp-tailed
Dusky	Hazel hen	Sharp-winged
Willow	Capercailzie	Spruce

Four of these are found in the UK, the Black, Red, Capercailzie and Ptarmigan. The most famous of them, indigenous only
to this country, is the Red *(Lagopus lagopus scoticus)*. It is a
subspecies of the circumpolar willow grouse *(Lagopus lagopus)*
which has several subspecies in other parts of the world. The red
grouse is distinctive in that it does not have white wings and
does not turn white, or mostly white, in winter. The voice and
behaviour of the different varieties are very similar. The red
grouse used to be regarded as a separate species but this idea has
been rejected for some years.

It is a truly wild bird which cannot be easily reared and
released like partridges and pheasants. This, of course, makes
life difficult for the host at a grouse shoot, or the agent letting a
moor to fee-paying Guns. He cannot say, or at least think to
himself, 'We've put down 4000 birds so by the time shooting
starts there must be at least 3000 or so of them around.'

Grouse have been reared in small numbers, but the first snag
in rearing them in quantity is, who will supply the eggs? Most
moor keepers wish to preserve every nest they can find. Since
experiments began at the end of the nineteenth century keepers

Grouse covey fly past, showing how sometimes it is easy inadvertently to shoot two birds with one shot

Aggressive grouse His red raised wattle makes him look especially fierce

St Mark's flies swarming over the moor as soon as the wind drops. Fortunately they do not bite people

have reared grouse and managed to feed the chicks on oatmeal and various greenstuffs, plus rearing-crumbs and some heather. When the young birds are released, however, the heather diet in the wild is often too tough for them and many starve. They also get driven away by the resident birds and become easy prey for predators.

Adult grouse can be caught in the wild and taken to areas where there are no birds, or only very few. They should survive for a while and could be shot, but they will not improve the breeding stock; that can only be done by looking after the moor: heather burning, controlling grazing, reducing the numbers of vermin.

Grouse weigh about 20 to 24 ounces, the cocks being a little heavier than the hens. A bird of 30 ounces or more is exceptional. Hens put on weight in the spring before laying, and indeed on their fitness at this time depends the quality of the eggs and chicks. Six to eight are usually laid, occasionally up to twelve, close to young edible heather about 4 inches high; the nest is in longer old heather where the brood can run for cover when disturbed. If the ground is heavily grazed by cattle, sheep or deer so that there is no tall heather for cover, grouse prefer not to nest there.

During the summer the young birds live with their parents, the family being called a covey. By August the old cocks start becoming aggressive, taking up position early in the day on prominent rocks or mounds and proclaiming their ownership of an area.

In October and November young and old cocks fight for territories; by this time the families have split up and birds which have not obtained a territory are driven away and join together in packs.

Soon all available territories are claimed and the successful cocks pair, sometimes with a young hen, sometimes an old one. The cocks defend their patch in the mornings and indulge in display flights, rising up steeply a few feet and descending while calling defiance. An old name for this is 'becking', derived from the sound they make. Later in the day most of the birds feed together and then form packs for the night. In hard winter weather they stay in packs all through the day.

By March the territory-owners are defending their land throughout the day and driving off any non-territorial birds. Many of the latter will have died from disease, starvation or predators; they are the real unfortunates who cannot breed unless they are lucky enough to take over a territory from an owner who has been killed by predators or had an accident such as flying into wires.

A good stock of breeding pairs in April would be one pair to 5 acres. It might increase to as much as one pair to 2 acres, or fall to one pair to 200 acres. The fluctuation depends on the size of the territories taken over by the cocks the previous autumn; this can vary considerably and seems to be Nature's way of controlling the grouse population according to food availability and other circumstances.

Healthy, well-fed hens produce good quality eggs and strong chicks. Poor quality eggs mean weak chicks, many of which die within their first week. Good breeding conditions follow a good, reasonably dry summer with not too severe a winter, and then a mild spring, giving plentiful early growth of heather.

In a very good year chicks will survive to form a covey of eight, plus the parents, by August: a young to adult ratio of 4 to 1. In a poor year this ratio may be only 1 to 1, and it can sink lower.

None of the birds has a great life expectation; two out of three alive in August will be dead a year later, whether they are shot or not. A bird that achieves a territory has a good chance of surviving for a year, but if it fails it will probably die that winter.

Most grouse do not move very far from the area where they are hatched, frequently not more than a mile. Claims that large packs have migrated long distances are often open to doubt; many mass movements are only temporary, caused by predators or hunger in severe weather.

Although heather *(Calluna vulgaris)* is the chief food, grouse eat the berries, flowers and seeds of a great many other plants. Bell heather *(Erica cinerea)* is not normally eaten except when it is in flower. The nutrient value of these plants is largely dependent on the richness of the soil, which again is influenced by the underlying rock; if this contains lime and is soft enough to break

Grit placed close to butt The butt has chestnut paling to keep off sheep and also safety posts each side to deter the Gun from shooting down the line

down fairly easily, the soil will be fertile and the plants contain
more potassium, nitrogen and mineral trace elements than those
growing on poor soil, provided that there is not too thick a layer
of peat for the plants' roots to reach through. Limestone in the
soil makes for good feeding and a strong grouse stock. (Some
people think it is for this same reason that horses do so well in
Ireland.)

Certain plants grow in rich soils while others flourish on fairly
infertile ones; in evaluating the potential of a moor to support
grouse, a botanist could be of considerable help by listing the
plants growing on it and so deducing the quality of the soil.

Some of the plants that provide food are:

blaeberry	bog myrtle
(sometimes called bilberry	heath rush
or whortleberry)	oat stubbles
crowberry	turnip leaves
cranberry	(occasionally)
cotton sedge	bearberry
cloudberry	crossleaved heath

Grouse also eat insects, although the young are not so dependent on them for protein as are partridge chicks.

Contrary to some beliefs grouse do drink and during incuba-
tion the hens visit the nearest pool or stream every day. In dry
weather all birds can take the early morning dew and in hard
weather snow crystals will suffice.

Having no teeth, birds must have grit in their gizzards to
grind up their food: grouse require especially tough, sharp grit
to deal with their heather diet. This grit is constantly being worn
smooth and needs regular replacement. White quartz is the best
and the birds need plenty of it, from when they are only a few
days old. Where there are hard rocks, such as granite, quartz will
be plentiful, but on moors covered by deep peat and with only
soft rocks, quartz will be at a premium. It can be brought in and
placed in small mounds in open places out on the moor where
the birds will soon find it. Being white it is conspicuous (see also
Chapter 4).

A certain amount of grit is also available to the birds from the
roads crossing the moor but this may not be sufficient. Many

people think it is particularly important to keep the birds supplied in winter and early spring when the heather is tougher and food intake for the hens is vital. Since snow may cover the birds' gritting place, keepers sometimes place quartz in boxes raised a few feet off the ground.

Grouse are remarkably talkative birds, at least the cocks are, especially when declaring their proprietorial rights. Everyone knows the much quoted 'Go back, go back, go back!' but the bird can say a lot more than that. And in any case that expression is really a misquote. Difficult though it may be to transpose grouse talk to the printed word, what he really says is more like 'Go bare, go bare, go bare'. Of course, there might be a slight difference between the accents of Yorkshire and Scottish grouse!

Some sportsmen who scarcely visit a grouse moor except to occupy a butt will not have heard many of the birds' utterances. If, however, you sit still and quiet near an area containing several birds you will probably hear something like this:

> 'Owk! – Urr, urr, urr erk.'
> 'Grrr, urk, urk, urk, urk.'
> 'Wairk! – Wairk! – Wairk!'
> 'Chk – Chk, chk, chk.'
> 'Cark, gug, gug, gug, gare.'

But you need to be another grouse to know what it all means! Although, in fact, researchers at the Institute of Terrestrial Ecology, Banchory, believe they have worked out what the calls signify. Hen grouse make a quieter, almost yelping sound.

Disease can seriously reduce the stock on a grouse moor. The main way of combating it is to avoid over-crowding and to ensure that the birds have plenty to eat. The chief attacks on their health come from coccidiosis, tapeworms, strongylosis and louping ill.

Coccidiosis is found in domestic poultry and in reared pheasants. It is caused by a parasite which the bird picks up and then passes in its droppings, so spreading the infection. It can affect grouse chicks but rarely kills many of them; adult birds are not often affected. Many grouse have tapeworms, but seldom with any ill effect. Both these complaints are likely to be seriously harmful only to birds which have been weakened first by semi-starvation.

Far more serious is strongylosis, commonly called 'grouse disease'. It is caused by the minute trichostrongyle threadworm *(Trichostrongylus tenuis)*. All over the moor there are grouse droppings containing threadworm eggs which during the winter cold remain dormant. With the warmth of spring they hatch and soon millions of larvae settle in the young heather shoots, ready to infect the birds, which have had a hard enough time surviving the winter.

The larvae climb up young green shoots of heather and, near the tip, enshroud themselves in a hard sheath; this both protects them from temporary dryness and from the cutting of the grit in the bird's gizzard. Having entered the intestine, the worms live off the host bird, mate and lay eggs. These are passed out in the droppings, the larvae hatch, look for another heather stem, and so the cycle goes on (one vital feature of this cycle is that the heather stem must be wet to enable the larva to climb it – prolonged drought will kill many of the larvae and also the eggs in the grouse's droppings before they have become larvae).

The more birds, the more disease they will encourage. Big stocks of grouse, therefore, foretell disaster: unless they are culled, and the best way of doing that is by shooting. A restrictive policy of 'leaving more to breed for next year' can result only in there being more birds to die during the winter, birds which might have been brought to bag during August and September, and more survivors to spread disease next year.

Most grouse are diseased although the majority of the worms are carried by a few heavily infected birds. So what can be done before the application of Nature's remedy? This is to kill off the majority of the birds, although it is now generally accepted that they are not so much killed by the disease as weakened to such an extent that they starve: the worm enters the caecum, or blind gut, into which digested food passes and when this is congested with thousands of tiny worms the wretched bird can no longer obtain enough nourishment.

Drastic falls in grouse populations may be caused by the

interaction of heather quality and infection by strongyle worms; this could influence body condition and affect territorial success and breeding.

The counter-action required is to keep up a good supply of young green heather shoots by efficient burning; to provide plenty of sharp grit at all times, so that the food can be digested; to keep the moor well drained, since the strongyle eggs cannot hatch in dry conditions; to keep down numbers of grouse.

The shooting policy can help considerably in keeping the disease in check. The object is to prevent grouse stocks building up too much which, though it may allow a gratifyingly big bag one year, will be followed by decimation by disease the next. There is a limit to the number of birds an area of ground can support, especially when they are to a certain extent protected by having their natural enemies reduced. This number will vary according to conditions such as height, climate, rainfall, fertility of soil and grazing policy for cattle and sheep. Determining the figure and striving to keep to it is one of the most important principles in good moor management.

For instance, if you have a poor hatching season you should probably still shoot normally, otherwise you will be sparing the old birds which could increase the infestation of the land. In a good breeding season you should shoot hard and late, again to account for as many old birds as possible, the theory being that they carry the most disease. Current research on grouse disease includes trials involving dosing wild birds with an anthelminthic and subsequently keeping track of them by radio.

In some years there is a poor showing of grouse in certain parts of the country whereas other places still have birds in considerable numbers, which puzzles a great many people. There may be many causes, and when they all apply at once, and perhaps for consecutive years, grouse numbers dwindle alarmingly and shooting has to stop. The reasons may be summarized:

1 Snow and frost in late spring.
2 Insufficient heather burning.
3 Over-grazing by subsidized sheep.
4 A reduction in the number of keepers.

5 A lack of ability and ignorance of grouse biology
  by some young keepers and factors.
6 Over-shooting after a bad breeding season.

The disease known as louping ill is a virus passed from one
animal to another by ticks *(Ixodes ricinus)*. Large parts of Scotland are affected by it, the disease being mainly carried by sheep,
and it was probably brought to the grouse moors when the
Highland sheep industry expanded in the nineteenth century.
Hares can also carry the ticks and so, too, can deer, both red and
roe, rabbits, voles and hedgehogs. Sheep dipping, when properly carried out, kills their ticks but of course nothing can be
done about wild hosts.

Ticks alone are not normally a serious danger but louping ill is
a killer, and most grouse affected by it die.

The favoured places for ticks to live are in the damp mat of
dead, undecomposed heather, grass and other plants on lightly
grazed moors at low altitude. This lends strength to the policy
of having good drainage on a moor, and of removing as much
bracken as possible.

In England ticks are noticeably less of a menace to grouse. A
shepherd in Wensleydale will tell you that it is because his sheep
are better fed than those in Scotland, and so become more
resistant to ticks. A less unlikely reason may be that the richer
mineral subsoil, producing more nutritious heather, makes for
fitter grouse able to survive the attentions of ticks; and also less
of the mat of dead grass etc. Certainly high-lying moors do not
have ticks and even heavily grazed ground in England has very
few.

The repetitive life story of these parasites starts with the
engorged female dropping off her host into the grass, where she
remains for about three weeks and then lays her eggs. These can
hatch in a month, or may take eight months if winter intervenes.
The larvae climb the stalks of herbage and attach themselves to
any passing animal or bird. They are replete in four days, when
they fall off and await ecdysis into the nymphal stage, which
again can take a few weeks or nine months, according to season.
Then up the stalks again, five days for engorgement, fall off and
three or four months for ecdysis to the adult stage. Once more

up the stalks, engorgement taking a week to ten days this time, and there is the adult ready to breed.

Any warm-blooded creature is acceptable to the tick which has no enemies preying on it. Eradication is difficult; even if land is cleared of sheep it can still carry a larval population.

The cure for louping ill? It all comes down to better moor management: removing the habitat favoured by ticks; ensuring (how difficult is this?) that tenant farmers carry out correct, regular and frequent sheep dipping; keeping the ground well drained. From the grouse's point of view the sheep should be dipped in early April, before the ticks can attack the chicks, although the farmer may claim that this interferes with lambing. Not all farmers are aware that a vaccine against louping ill is now available for sheep; if used properly it could eliminate the disease in grouse.

Apart from the diseases which can sicken or kill poor old lagopus, he and his mate are most extraordinarily hardy birds. Living, for preference, on high ground, he nearly always has to endure a snowy winter, but he is adept at getting through the snow to his food. In conditions of hard frost grouse will often follow deer or cattle whose weight is sufficient to break through the icy crust. The hen bird is extremely persevering when brooding her eggs, and will remain on the nest even in continuous torrential rain, almost enough to wash the eggs out of the nest. A case is on record of a keeper actually treading on a brooding hen, so tight was she sitting. He was more scared than the poor bird, which escaped with the loss of a feather or two and one broken egg. The birds are amazingly tolerant of adverse weather; they can even tread down the snow during a night blizzard so as to avoid being buried. Half-grown chicks, however, are vulnerable to wet and cold when they are too big to be protected by the mother and not quite strong enough to look after themselves.

The migration of grouse is a vexed subject, accepted by some people, regarded by others as mostly just a keeper's excuse for not having many birds on his beat. Generally speaking, grouse sometimes move down from higher to lower ground in a hard winter, returning the following spring, but they seldom migrate considerable distances, except to find better ground with more food. This is less likely in England than in the Highlands of Scotland where, in exceptionally severe weather, huge packs may work their way south searching for food; survivors may lose their bearings and fail to return in the spring. Thus a moor may be denuded of its birds. Immigration, on the other hand, can benefit a moor which has lost its stock owing to a violent outbreak of disease, but which still offers good feeding.

Curiously, there are authenticated stories of grouse having been seen flying extraordinarily high, even of their flying out to sea or being found on the ground so exhausted that they could scarcely move, as if they had just flown an exceptionally long way. But mostly the birds are sedentary, rarely moving more than a few miles from where they are hatched, though occasionally they may vacate an area in July or August in an inexplicable manner. The grouse surely is a bird of mystery.

Here are some factors governing grouse behaviour:

1 The aggressive behaviour of cock grouse determines the number of birds living on a moor. Successful cocks grab a territory in the autumn and defend it against rivals; hens arrive and pair up with them; the unsuccessful birds nearly all die during the winter. The size of a territory varies with the amount of heather available, and then its quality, and perhaps the severity of the cock's aggressiveness.
2 Egg production is dependent on plenty of young green heather at the end of the winter. A well-fed hen produces a large clutch and strong chicks; on a poor diet her chicks are weak and many quickly die.
3 Grouse are selective feeders, able to select heather shoots rich in nitrogen and phosphorus.
4 Ground above lime-rich rocks grows more nutritive heather and other plants eaten by grouse, than that over granite.
5 Grouse are able to restrict or expand their numbers in two ways:
   (a) When food has been scarce the young birds in the autumn take over bigger territories than the old birds; in years of plenty the young take smaller areas.
   (b) They change the sex ratio in the breeding stock: in

good years equal numbers of both sexes mate, but in poor
years or when numbers have become excessive, some hens
fail to pair, thus reducing the numbers of broods in the
summer.

6 If heavy stocks of sheep or cattle continuously graze the
hill, with no rest period or rotational plan, the amount and
quality of the food available is much reduced, at the expense of both beasts and grouse.

7 The best way to increase the grouse population on a moor is
by efficient, well-planned heather burning, followed by
predator control.

8 Migration is a rare occurrence, usually caused by exceptional weather, or bad management; it can, however, affect
the grouse cycles of abundance and decline which occur
whether or not the moor is well managed.

The blackcock *(Lyurus tetrix britannicus)*, whose real colour is
a steely blue and purple, has a handsome lyre-shaped tail,
startling white under-tail coverts, and a bright scarlet wattle
over each eye. The female is called a greyhen, although she is
mostly brown with black transverse bars. In their choice of
habitat and food they favour a wider variety of conditions than
the red grouse.

When they eat young shoots of pine and larch, black grouse
are not popular with foresters, but they also frequent grasslands,
open moors, roots and stubbles, taking insects, buds (especially
of birch), seeds, and berries as well as heather shoots, the
predominant diet of red grouse. They prefer woods with good
ground cover for nesting, and they are more likely to be found
on the fringes of moors rather than far out in open country.

The particularly fascinating feature of the species is the display of the males at the communal ground known as the lek; this
word is said to derive from a Norse verb 'laika' meaning to play,
jump or tremble; very apt. The lek is a flat area, usually with
short grass, of varying size, perhaps about 50 by 30 yards; it may
be a clearing among trees, or at the edge of a wood or some way
out on the open fell. It is a traditional ground and the same spot
may be used for fifty years or more; even if it is ploughed up the
birds will try to occupy the same area.

Blackcock at the lek Each bird occupies quite a small area but immediately attacks any other which crosses the boundary

Blackcock The bird displays and utters the 'Tschoo-ee' call

Ptarmigan in late summer plumage

The blackcock assemble at dawn a few hundred yards away from the lek and begin walking, running and finally flying in a scramble to reach their appointed places. Each has a small territory on which he displays, with tail fanned out, white under-feathers erect, wings partly spread and drooping, and scarlet wattles swollen; he also makes frequent rushes to attack any bird which crosses his boundary. The performance has distinct phases, which have been interpreted as follows.

First, the crowing, when the cock stands up, holds his head high and utters a strange double note of which the first syllable is like a mixture between a soda-water siphon and a sneeze: 'Tschoo-wee!' He also jumps a couple of feet into the air every now and then, the purpose of the sneeze-and-jump manoeuvre being to advertise the lek to the hens.

Second, the note uttered as the cocks rush at each other, a sort of 'Kokker-arr'. There is much mock bravado in their posturing, one bird running back as the other advances, and then immediately the roles are reversed. Wings flap, beaks may occasionally clash and breasts bump, but very little damage results from these sparring matches on territorial boundaries.

Third, the song, that aggressive, possessive call by which most birds advertise what they regard as their ownership of territory. Here the cock bends forward, stretches his neck and distends the throat pouches; with his whole body quivering and feathers trembling he utters the 'Roo koo roo, roo *koor*-you' cry over and over again.

Usually, after about half an hour the birds calm down and start preening. Then one of them shouts, 'Tschoo-wee!' and this infectious sound starts them all off again; as of course does the appearance of a hen, although very often throughout the entire two- or three-hour performance at the lek no hens appear at all.

When a hen does decide to drop in she walks into the arena and appears to eye the boys in turn to see if one takes her fancy. As she passes down the lines all the males display madly, with heads held low and tails high; she may crouch in front of one, which is the mating signal, and the cock then circles her and mounts. She may continue right through the lek and fly away. The cocks then seem open to the criticism of all pose and no performance!

In fact, the hens appear only during the mating time, late April and early May, while the display period may last from mid-March until mid-June. There is also frequently an afternoon session and also a return visit, cocks only, no hens and no sexual activity, in the autumn. The rarity of seeing a hen on the lek has given rise to some curious myths about the mating methods of blackgame, especially among countrymen, including gamekeepers, who have never had time to sit in a hide and watch developments. One such belief is that the birds mate orally, with the cock spitting into the hen's mouth.

The reason for the long periods which the cocks spend at the lek interests ornithologists and those who love to speculate on such matters. It appears that the original function of the display was purely sexual, calling the hens in to a meeting place of the polygamous cocks; certainly the roo-kooing sound, which has an insistent rhythm, like a wood pigeon's, carries a long way. The strictly defined territorial boundaries reduce interference from other males during copulation, and the fighting ensures that only the fittest birds succeed in mating. A secondary function of the lek is probably a social one, a kind of tribal dance such as those performed by primitive peoples.

Blackgame are bigger than grouse, the cock weighing 3 or 4 pounds and the hen about a pound less. Because of their size and fairly slow-looking wingbeat they are easily missed, the shooter failing to realize that in fact they usually fly faster than grouse. People not used to seeing them often mistake them for duck. As they are fairly rare the greyhen is normally given unofficial protection and not shot. On estates where the birds are reasonably plentiful this can be a mistake, as it may result in the survival of a lot of crabby old barren hens who chase off the up-and-coming fertile virgins.

The caper *(Tetrao urogallus)* is the biggest of the grouse. You may spell him capercaillie, or capercailzie: the intruding 'z' can have a certain attraction because it is not pronounced anyway, coming from the old Scots 'z' which was pronounced like the 'y' in 'you'. The name derives from the Gaelic for 'Horse of the Wood', and at 10 pounds weight or more it suits him.

Although almost as big as a turkey this bird, when driven

from a hillside pinewood in winter, bursts out noisily and then flies fast, high and silently; it presents a startling and well worthwhile target for the sportsman. The birds are apt to be unpopular with foresters because of their liking for artificially raised conifer seedbeds, where they eat the young shoots.

The cocks perform a courtship display in the spring, somewhat similar to the blackcock. Their weird song at that time has been likened to the pop of a cork being pulled out of a bottle, with peculiar scratching rattles.

The prettiest and most charming member of the grouse family is the ptarmigan *(Lagopus mutus)*. Much of its attraction arises from the fact that it lives much higher than the red grouse, above 2000 feet and up to over 4000 feet; it sees very little of man, the arch-predator, and so confides in him to the extent of sometimes walking around, almost unconcernedly, within a few yards.

Even if you go high enough you may easily miss a sighting because of the ptarmigan's excellent camouflage, blending marvellously with the pale grey rocks, white spar and speckled dried moss. With apparently no cover except a few stones it is almost invisible when standing still, and is very difficult to spot as it creeps ahead of an intruder. If it crouches and shuts its eyes, and you look away for a second, the bird can magically disappear, until it opens its eyes again. Then, as so often happens with an animal's otherwise perfect disguise, the shine of a beady eye reveals it.

When it flies the ptarmigan often swings out over the valley rather than hugging the contour line, like a grouse. A covey suddenly springing from their sanctuary among the rocks is like an explosion of big white butterflies. Scattering and weaving away from the mountain, the birds make a difficult shot, except for the fact that, if they have not previously been harried, they may delay their departure until the shooter is practically standing among them. As the birds are so trusting it does seem rather a shame to shoot them in this way. When driven they make more difficult shots. Most owners of ptarmigan hills restrict the numbers that are shot; the birds are excellent eating, they fly just as fast as grouse, and so, in limited quantities, are no mean prize.

How does the bird survive? Mostly by living in reasonably inaccessible places, above the generally expected range of fox and hooded crow; it is still sometimes a prey to them and also to the golden eagle, from whom its only protection is its colouring: brownish in summer, grey and black in autumn and white in winter. Incidentally, the bird's well-feathered legs and toes are no mere ornament, but are a considerable help in walking over snow. Pheasant, grouse and woodcock have heather and grass and bracken in which to conceal themselves, which makes all the more remarkable the manner in which ptarmigan can hide in their bare habitat; their whole behaviour is aimed at survival against predators.

The ptarmigan is the only British game bird with white wings. Even in its summer plumage one is reminded that this is a bird which has a hardy existence all year round. Living near the top of a Scottish mountain, it survives the snows of winter and rears its young even in a wet, cold and windy spring. The hen is a devoted mother and will 'attack' a man who walks close to her brood, and then entice him away by walking ahead, often looking back as if to make sure he is following, until she has led him well away from her chicks.

The birds feed on ling, bilberry, crowberry, cloudberry and, occasionally, lichens and mosses, although on first seeing their terrain you might be excused for wondering how they find sufficient sustenance at all. Entrancing as they are to watch, and admirable in their habits, their voice can scarcely be called beautiful; it is a sort of guttural croak and crick, disappointingly unsuitable to their grace.

A bird of the lower moorland, and one which appears quite often on a grouse shooting day, is the snipe. Pushed off some little boggy patch by the beaters it flitters over the Guns, higher than most of them are looking and a bit perplexing because it is so *small*. Sometimes a few are added to the bag; they are difficult to find when they have fallen into deep heather, but make an excellent breakfast served on fried bread with grilled bacon.

A grouse drive often takes quite a long time, longer than inexperienced Guns expect, especially when the beaters are still moving out to their start line while the Guns are already in their butts. When the beaters do get nearer, even though they are still out of sight, the occupants of the butts may become aware of a charm of finches swooping and bobbing about, uttering their small, sibilant cries. They are the first birds, the advance guard and a warning to be ready for the grouse in a moment or two. Other small birds commonly seen around the moor are meadow pipit, stonechat, and wheatear.

Sometimes, unfortunately, it may be a different bird that appears first: a golden eagle. This handsome predator can clear a moor of grouse because they simply fly away on its approach, knowing that it kills on the ground rather than on the wing. A visiting hen harrier can have much the same effect. Some current thinking suggests that hen harriers might be taken off the protected list, at least under licence. Their numbers might then be reduced, to the great benefit of grouse, perhaps by the use of the narcotic alphachloralose, in the same way that the Royal Society for the Protection of Birds controls herring gulls. Culling any animal or bird frequently rouses indignation, usually among people unaware of all the facts, but it is done at the expense of a majority to save a minority.

Kestrels, sparrowhawks and peregrines occasionally take grouse but as birds of prey they also are protected. Although the buzzard is too slow to be a direct threat, it may be mistaken for a golden eagle, causing the grouse to make a hasty departure and so ruin a drive.

Birds of far less grace and of considerable danger are carrion crows, hooded crows and gulls. They steal eggs as well as chicks, and also attack weakly lambs, pecking out their eyes and tongues; even ewes, when cast on their backs and unable to get up, are vulnerable. The moor keeper wages continual war against them. Another egg stealer and killer of young birds is the largest member of the crow family, the raven, which is protected; not all its activities are harmful, however, and it does some good by clearing away carrion.

The remaining flying inhabitants of the moor are the insects, which generally frequent damp marshy patches. They are taken by grouse and although apparently not an essential item of diet they are popular with newly hatched chicks. Best known of these flying furies is the midge *(Culcoides impunctatus)* which lurks unseen on windy days and attacks with an apparently insatiable blood lust as soon as the wind drops. No one who has not experienced an attack by these devils can possibly imagine how frightful it is. There appear to be more of them in Scotland than in the south, and picnickers and salmon fishers are sometimes driven frantic, being forced to give up and retreat to their cars, while campers can be seen hurrying hysterically to the nearest town for anti-sting lotions. If you don't believe this, and think it is an exaggeration, wait till you find yourself in a grouse butt one fine day, when suddenly the breeze falls away and you discover that you are close to a nice, wet, midge-encouraging bog.

More interesting are the St Mark's flies. They live in the heather, are occasionally eaten by grouse and do not bite humans. They are noticeable because they are so large, and they appear when the wind eases, rising and falling like the swarms of spinners that trout fishermen view with happy anticipation when they see them over a river. These flies hang their long legs down in a curious way, looking like old-fashioned aeroplanes with non-retractable undercarriages. Crane flies, the well known daddy-longlegs, are also on the grouse's menu.

Up on the hill, then, are all those fascinating birds; but of course our main interest is centred on the red grouse. With conservation so popular these days, much is done to look after the bird, and inevitably at times it becomes too numerous, until Nature steps in and devastates the numbers with disease and foul weather.

Mostly the harvest is safely gathered in and the birds go to market, often to be sold for exorbitant prices in restaurants. Roast young grouse, probably the most tasty of all game birds, is a marvellous dish when prepared properly and simply.

How do we know which is an old bird and which a young? Most of the traditional methods of ageing them are not very accurate. Some people will tell you to hold up a grouse by its lower mandible, which will break if the bird is a young one: this is not accurate except with very young birds, and well-grown birds of that year will often have strong enough jaws to withstand the test by September. A similar test involves crushing the bird's skull with one's thumb, but this is also uncertain with a well-developed young bird.

Many keepers examine the birds' nails, looking for signs: a nail half off means an old bird, which normally sheds its nails about July and August; a scar across the top of a new nail shows where the old one was, therefore it is an old bird; transverse ridges across even a new nail mean an old bird, while longer, smoother claws indicate a young one.

Another easy, quick and popular way of distinguishing the ages is to look at the third outermost primary wing feather. In a young bird this will be shorter than the others. But this is not a 100 per cent test, because sometimes a well-developed young bird, especially in a year when the hens were able to nest early, will have grown its third primary as long as the others. And occasionally in a late year an old hen may have moulted late and not have acquired a full set of new primaries by mid-August.

Checking the feathers can help, though, if you look at the tips of the two outer primaries. An old bird's have rounded tips whereas a young one's have pointed tips, frequently with very small ginger spots. The moult problem, however, can arise again because you might find one of last year's birds which has still not moulted these two feathers: they will still look pointed though they will also be worn and faded. Really accurate ageing is difficult without experience; if you want to apply these tests seriously you should seek a little practical instruction from an expert, who probably uses all of them plus a look at the general appearance of the plumage.

One certain method of detecting a young bird is to examine its vent. Alongside the excretory cavity is a blind tube called the bursa, into which, if the bird is young, you can *gently* push a matchstick to the depth of about 1 inch. This strange sort of pouch remains open until the following spring; if you cannot probe easily into it with your match, the bird is an old one.

The red grouse is a superlative bird and from the sportsman's point of view has no peer. Of all game birds it is the most difficult shot and the best to eat. Recipes do not have to be complicated but are worth learning from an expert such as Robert Carrier or André Simon, who wrote that the grouse is 'the best of all game birds in the world'.

Old and young grouse The third primary of the top bird, in the man's left hand, is shorter than those on either side

The basic factor in cooking the birds is to appreciate the great difference between young and old. Both must be hung, for up to two weeks in the cooler weather of October, although four or five days is probably enough for a young bird in August. They should be hung in a fly-proof place, and if they have to be transported for a day or two in a car it is no bad thing to give them a squirt with a fly-repellent spray.

With a young bird you cannot do better than roast it, putting a knob of butter inside and perhaps some cranberries. Like most game, the birds are dry and need basting or larding, which means placing bacon over the breasts or, better still, strips of fat salt pork in the French way.

This is a gourmet's dish and needs very little accompaniment. French beans, redcurrant or rowan jelly go well with it and a salad of watercress, tarragon and lettuce. Each bird should be placed on a piece of toast or crouton of fried bread on to which fall the drippings while it roasts. Other gravies and sauces are quite unnecessary. Cooking time is twenty-five minutes to half an hour at 450°F. It must not be underdone, not at all sanglant when carved.

An old recipe of the 1890s must surely have been aimed at gourmands when it suggested that grouse needed to be preceded by 'only' soup, fish and *one* entrée. A slightly more modern Scottish recipe instructs the cook to stuff the bird with heather trimmings and roast it on a beech board, kept specially for this dish and not washed between usages.

It may be that one is lucky enough to be sent a brace of grouse; if they have not travelled well and appear to be horribly high do not despair. They are not bad, just a little ripe. Plucking them may be messy but if they are washed in a weak solution of vinegar they will almost certainly be perfectly edible.

Old birds, alas, are terribly disappointing if they are just roasted. They need to be casseroled, or braised; the meat is then taken off the bones, pounded up with the breast fillets, and made into soup.

Claret, of course, goes excellently with grouse, and gooseberry fool is as good a pudding as any to follow. It is worth remembering, too, that the bird is particularly tasty when eaten cold.

Ptarmigan and blackgame can be cooked as red grouse, although they are rarely mentioned in the cook books. Even less often included is the capercailzie. Because it eats pine shoots, the caper is strong-flavoured and some people claim the taste is no better than chewing a turpentine-soaked rag! The vital point is that the bird must be well hung, like a wild goose – three weeks is not too long – and the crop and pine needles removed. Of course, some faddy feeders say that you should bury it in the garden and then forget where you buried it! André Simon says it should be stewed slowly for two hours.

Not much else that comes off the moor, except a snipe or two, is likely to appear on the table. There is the possibility of a hare, although often they are not shot, partly for safety reasons. The brown hare of England and the Scottish lowlands is well enough known to the recipe writers to appear in most of their books, but the blue hare, which changes to white in the winter, rarely has a mention. It can be made appetizing, however, if cut up and placed in a marinade of Madeira, olive oil, vinegar, shallots, herbs and black pepper where it must remain for a week, the joints being turned daily. Then the pieces should be fried until well browned, braised with chestnuts and served with crabapple jelly. The left-overs can also be used by taking the flesh from the bones, pounding it up in a mortar with herbs and butter, and rubbing it through a sieve to make pâté.

A young grouse is so delectable a bird that the very simplest cooking will suffice to make a succulent dish. Cook it in a closed pan, having browned the bird in butter, with a cup of red wine, seasoning and a few shallots. It should be done slowly for half an hour, or even five minutes longer, and then eaten with brown bread dunked in the gravy, and some golden French beans. The memory of the sensuous pleasure of sucking off the last remnants of flesh from the bones will linger longer than recollections of far grander banquets. Especially if you cooked it like that while camping.

3 The People

'The blast-off of guns for the Glorious Twelfth heralds the start of another privileged season of licensed game slaughter for the trigger-happy, well-heeled sportsman.'

Certain sections of the Press seem incapable of greeting the grouse shooting season except by such claptrap. Often the inaccurate reports go further than this quote, with reference to the 'popping of rifles' and to people 'enjoying the grouse shooting scene in Suffolk'.

Without taking up cudgels with the anti-field sports brigade about shooting as a whole, one wonders why writers have to include so many astonishing insults against the people who go grouse shooting. 'Sick, sadistic morons', 'short fat peer' and 'chinless wonder' are often derisively applied to those fortunate enough to be sufficiently well off to shoot grouse. And deliberately provocative words are used, so that a bird is not shot, but 'slaughtered', when it becomes a 'limp bundle of feathers'.

It is curious. Most of us are a bit envious of those who have more money, but when the objects of envy are in showbiz, or perhaps big biz, they are called the 'jet set' and followed by admiring journalists pounding out superlative epithets concerning their beauty and skill and esoteric way of life.

If you want to shoot driven grouse in the cream of the season you have to spend a lot of money. It is like going ocean racing, owning a racehorse, driving a Mercedes or living in the Ritz. So what is wrong with anyone who can afford it going grouse shooting? Why should he be called 'tweedy' in an oddly derogative way, and be insulted about his physical appearance?

'Grouse shooting has become an absurdly ritualized myth,' squeaks a correspondent to a provincial newspaper, for any article on the subject prompts much free copy in the form of letters to the editor. In fact, the shooting is much less ritualized than it used to be and it never was a myth.

As well as insults, articles sometimes offer strange information and instruction on such non-subjects as the way keepers rear the birds: snippets like the keeper in springtime hoping for fine weather, 'with no thunderstorms to burst the grouse's eggs'. And here is something on butt positioning: 'Grouse butts are so sited that the shot can be well spread out and there is no fear of a low-flying bird being riddled with shot.' The reader is left pondering on how the location of the butts has any effect on the density of the shot pattern.

It just could be that some of the misinformation, as distinct from spiteful cavilling, is the result of tongue-in-cheek leg-pulling by the original informant. The late Tim Sedgwick, when he was editor of *The Shooting Times*, used to delight in telling gullible journalists in pubs such heresies as 'wild geese return to their nests each night', and 'buzzards make excellent eating'.

Much of the Press seems not to like the people on the grouse moors, but very little harm is done by the reports.

Nearly all of the land on which grouse flourish is private and many of the owners inherited their holding. Before the 1939–45 war shoots were mostly private, and before the Great War custom allowed the landed gentry and the aristocracy considerable freedom in running their shoots pretty much as they wished. Now economic circumstances have forced landowners to let their shooting to strangers, or at least to offer a welcome to paying guests. Of course, there has to be a drill for running a shoot, for efficiency and for safety, but it is far from a solemn observance of archaic procedures.

It is all more democratic now and although milord may have his own house-party shooting for a week or so before he lets his moors, the atmosphere is by no means forelock-touching feudalism. Mutual respect is apparent at all levels, and indeed if this were lacking the day would become extremely difficult to run.

A member of the nobility, a first class shot, is seen berating his dog after the drive, for some misdemeanour. Dog slinks away.

'Sit!' roars its owner running after it and trying to whack it with a long shepherd's crook stick.

Dog retreats. 'Sit!' Dog sits.

The stick is raised. Dog retreats.

'Sit!' Dog sits.

Up stick, Dog away.

Owner notices a small group of beaters standing watching.

'I think he's got more sense than I thought he had!' he says.

One of the group: 'But 'ee don't shoot so straight, me Lord!'

A most respected newspaper showed a picture taken at a research station of a grouse. Caption: 'This bird was specially reared to be shot in the field.' A less well known journal, oblivious of the fact that the birds cannot be reared and released like pheasants: 'Grouse are hand reared by keepers, and by the time they get to the moor they are so fat and stupid they can barely see, let alone fly.'

From unheeding ignorance come these wildly inaccurate statements aimed at stirring up distaste for grouse shooters. It is a weird brand of prejudice against the 'tweedy company' and almost always based on lack of knowledge coupled with no attempt to find out the truth. An accomplished writer well versed in field sports, Colin Willock, once summed it up as if some editor had asked him to 'write an article on the slalom prospects for the next Winter Olympics. I know less than nothing on the subject, but then I'd probably take the trouble at least to find out what they hit the ball with.'

The modern grouse shooting scene is a considerable hotch-potch of people, often with widely differing personalities; some pay, some are paid, all are there because they enjoy it, and through the generosity of the landowner; he in turn depends to a greater or lesser extent on the tolerance of his tenant farmers and shepherds.

The visitors often stay in nearby hotels which may have varied standards of comfort and service, although they usually try their best to oblige clients. One such hostelry from the past was described by Sir Ralph Payne-Gallwey, author of several shooting books and some fascinating game books and diaries. An entry for 1888 concerns a party of shooting gentlemen staying at a country inn. It seems that in their private dining room a decanter of sherry stood upon the sideboard. Although none of them drank any the level of sherry was lower each day. Suspecting the waiter they decided to play a clever trick on him: one of them topped up the decanter with a curious and personal liquid of the right amber shade. The decanter still became emptier and when they left they accused the waiter of stealing. 'Indeed, I never touched a drop,' he replied, 'I merely obeyed the cook's instructions and put two spoonfuls in your soup every night.'

Those who do the shooting today are not by any means always rich or aristocratic although some are both and many neither. On most shoots that let Guns, or shooting days, the customers a little later in the season are often groups of friends from the south, who pay comparatively little for their sport. They may be farmers or factory workers, and from whatever walk of life they come they are welcome on the hill. Often they are very good shots and well versed in country lore. Even if they lack experience in grouse shooting they are almost always keen to learn.

This particularly applies to foreign visitors. Many of them come year after year but there are always a number of newcomers and all of them experience a degree of language difficulty, even if it is only with local pronunciation of what should be familiar words.

A happy Frenchman with one party spoke no English at all. Before each drive he used to walk about holding up fingers, eyebrows raised and a quizzical expression on his face; it served well as a way of asking where his butt was.

When one of the Guns says, 'Some schoolies came over the blind but I was shooting like a plumber,' it is pretty obvious that he is one of Uncle Sam's sons. And a wish to give sympathetic assistance is the first reaction to his earlier question, 'Do they blow a horn to start things? I've never been on a grouse moor before.'

The old hands, full of experience, are the beaters and the flankers. The latter should not just be old retainers, getting deaf and too halt to walk long distances. A flanker, sometimes called a 'pointsman' in England, though the word is tending to go out of favour now, has to be alert, watch intelligently what is happening during a drive, and then spring into action to surprise the birds and turn them from their course and back towards the butts.

The beaters may be workers from the estate, although nowadays many of them are students from university or technical college, or even quite young schoolchildren, including girls. They have a tough day walking 12 or 15 miles over thick heather up steep rocky slopes, across slippery hillsides covered with bilberry. They may be soaked to the skin one day and then, when there is a heatwave, the young ones turn up in skimpy shorts and T-shirts and look like boiled lobsters by the end of the day. Naturally the regular beaters, assistant keepers and estate men, always dress the same, in Scotland in the laird's plaid if they have got it, and, as true Scots, appear impervious to all extremes of weather. How they can walk, some of those stalwarts! With the long steady stride of the mountain man, they cover the ground effortlessly without even getting out of breath.

It used to be customary to use the term 'drivers', but since the turn of the century 'beaters' has become more acceptable. About thirty beaters are needed for grouse driving and sometimes two lines are used. This speeds up the drives because one line can be moving into position while the other is actually doing a drive. All of them need flags, now usually made from the ubiquitous plastic fertilizer bag. These flags make a fine cracking noise when briskly waved, indicating clearly to the Guns where the beaters are. The cost of beaters is a big item in the expenses of the shoot. In 1986 the going rate was about £11 a day and, although some head keepers pay the boys only half wages, others pay the full rate – 'As long as the lads do what they're told. After all, they walk just as far as the men.'

Then there are the dog men, the pickers-up. They can be neighbouring keepers or local enthusiasts wanting to bring on young dogs, and give them experience of the real thing after weeks of training with dummies. Some are not so local, many dog owners travelling long distances from their homes in the

Loaders and pickers-up wait for the Guns Note the GSP among the dogs

Beaters and flankers The backbone of the shoot, who really know the ground and can assist the overworked keeper

south to have a few days picking-up in the north. It is very good experience for the dogs, too, because the open country means that dog and handler are within sight of one another practically all the time. This also means that everyone can see if the dog misbehaves and gallops off in the opposite direction to that indicated by its hopefully whistling owner!

Professional handlers who run their charges in Field Trials frequently bring three or four dogs to the moors, and what a joy it is to see them working each in turn while the others sit patiently and watch, each no doubt certain *it* could find that bird in a jiffy if given the chance. The picker-up is a wage-earning member of the team, although sometimes an owner-handler may prefer to concentrate on his dog, especially in its early training, and retain his amateur status.

Pickers-up usually stand well back behind the butts, out of range and possibly in a dip in the ground. Even there they are not always out of danger. An irate picker-up was once seen cursing and jumping up and down with rage, though fortunately not seriously hurt, shouting, 'I've been shot!' Most indignant he was, especially as he had been standing out of sight of the Guns. Out of sight, however, was not out of shot. Several of the party, acting on some extremely spurious advice, had armed themselves with heavy-load, high-velocity cartridges. These were sufficiently powerful, when fired behind at a low elevation, to carry some pellets over the crest behind which stood our picker-up, and administer a mild peppering!

The advantage of the pickers-up standing well back is that they can watch birds which fly on after being hit, and then fall a few hundred yards or perhaps half a mile behind the butts. Many are added to the bag in this way.

Among the birds that fly on, only to fall eventually, are those that perform that odd act called 'towering'. In this the bird flies almost vertically up; one explanation is that it has been hit in the lung and throws its head back as it struggles for air. Indeed, several reasons for this behaviour have been suggested and some people say that tower birds, when they fall in the open, are always found on their backs.

When pair guns are used a loader accompanies the shooter, his job being to keep his boss continuously supplied with a loaded gun during a drive. After the shooter fires he passes the gun to his loader, receiving in exchange another loaded gun (the drill for this is described in Chapter 6). Often loaders accompany the shooters even when single guns are being used, in order to help carry the gun and cartridges, and to pop cartridges quickly into the breech when the shooter opens his gun. Two guns and seventy-five cartridges weigh about 22 pounds, which can be quite a burden to carry up steep and slippery slopes. Lucky the shooter who can stroll along to his butt carrying no more than a stick, while his loader resembles a pack mule, encumbered with waterproof clothing as well as weapons, and such small useful gadgets as a cartridge extractor and a pair of binoculars.

When the loader does not 'belong' to his Gun, i.e. when he is supplied by the estate to a fee-paying visitor, he can probably be a help by explaining the lie of the land and the expected behaviour of the grouse. The visitor, however, should be a little cautious about the accuracy of the information being passed to him; the loader may be a terrific enthusiast, determined to do well in his unaccustomed job, but sadly lacking in experience. It is, of course, essential to make sure that the loader knows the functioning of the guns to be used; if he does not it sounds a warning that he may not know much about the job of loading either, and practice of the correct drill is indicated.

Startlingly dangerous behaviour by loaders sometimes takes place although it is seldom observed. Most of it emanates from the loader's desire to watch what is going on instead of concentrating on keeping a loaded gun held safely and ready to be taken. A loader who stands staring at the birds in the sky while holding a gun horizontal is a real menace, but not as uncommon as you might think.

An efficient loader is a great asset, a professional proud of doing a job well. But the enthusiastic amateur is the one of whom the visitor needs to be wary. (There's a corollary here somewhere.) Indeed, loading is a fine job: you do not have to walk miles like the beaters, you see all the fun of the shoot and you may be allowed to bring your dog and do some picking-up between drives. It is, however, a responsible job with a very important bearing on safety, and is not one to be entrusted to

A lady in a butt Sitting at the back and keeping low, she is out of the way when the Gun wants to shoot behind. Here he has just got a bird in front

Walking out to the butts The Guns party moves off on a fine August morning

any little-known volunteer whose chief desire may be some easily earned pay.

Good-looking clothes, on the grouse moor like everywhere else, have taken a retrograde step in recent years. You do not *have* to dress correctly but you have a duty to your host to be dressed in a reasonably smart and clean manner; on paying-guest shoots an amazing motley of casual gear appears. People wear skeet vests and primrose-coloured trousers, sky-blue shirts and red boots. The essence of correct wear is that it should be a fairly dark tone, blend with the surroundings and cover the wearer's head. Bright colours are said to turn the birds, and a pale moon-like blob which is the human face is the worst of all! So-called 'camouflage' jackets, which may be effective in a dappled woodland setting, only look conspicuous out on the moor.

A tweed shooting suit is best, and it is useful to have some thin stockings for use in hot weather at the beginning of the season. Thick winter stockings make one's feet far too hot in August. Clothes have to be suitable for walking as well as just sitting pretty in a grouse butt, so footwear, which should be non-slip, becomes very important.

Studded brogues are the standard. Very fine they look: good handsome leather, and comfortable. But they do need cleaning. Gum boots with studs are also a good bet, and more easily cleaned, Royal Hunters being the best. The point is that foot-wear has to be waterproof since a good deal of the moor is surprisingly wet. The alternative is just to accept wet feet for the sake of lightness, particularly when walking-up and when climbing to the heights for ptarmigan. Then some form of hockey boot or training shoe is suitable, even if singularly unsmart.

Because of extremes of weather, even in August, clothing may have to include gloves, jerseys and waterproof over-trousers and jackets, although some of it can be left in the transport. Conditions may be very cold indeed 2000 feet up with a strong wind hurtling down from the north. When the BBC weather forecaster says, 'Fine and warm in the south, with temperatures perhaps dropping to 70 degrees,' it sounds quite nice, but then he goes on, 'Scotland: showers, heavy in places,

winds fresh to strong, persistent rain spreading from the west
. . .' which can turn out to mean howling gales, rain like
stair-rods, and some cold and sodden grouse shooters.

The waxed-cotton types of waterproof jackets are very good
and are made in different weights (despite the weather mentioned in the previous paragraph, you do not need the
heavyweight, wildfowling type for grouse shooting). Barbours
of South Shields are pre-eminent as makers of clothing in this
material, which is quiet and does not rustle as the wearer
moves.

An efficient and really waterproof coat which can be rolled up
into a small bundle about 9 × 3 inches is the Bradsport Mountain Coat by Hebden Cord, of Hebden Bridge. Although it
rustles and has a hood (no good for shooters) it is so easily
carried that it becomes an almost essential piece of equipment.
Never wear a hood when shooting, you will not be able to hear
the birds.

When the weather is foul everyone looks much the same:
shapeless lumps, mostly dark green, swaddled in whatever
form of waterproof the sportswear shop salesman persuaded
them was best. But when the sun shines and the party becomes
recognizable as individuals it does, as it were, give the ladies a
chance to show their differences. Their hats, sometimes
adorned with badges, grouse-claw brooches and tufts of white
heather, need not be as austere as the caps and deerstalkers
generally favoured by males, though some modern-minded
men prefer the American western hat, made of leather and so
heavy and snug fitting that it stays on in strong winds; a curious
reciprocation of ideas since American visitors are often eager to
adopt the proven British forms of dress, the most discerning
even patronizing West End tailors.

A tweed suit, fairly loose-fitting jacket and knickerbockers,
variously called breeks or plus twos, is without doubt the
smartest wear, and a good tailor-made suit worn by a lady is
very attractive indeed. Even if shirt and jersey are substituted for
the tweed jacket, the knickerbockers are in every way preferable
to trousers, for both sexes, and corduroy or loden cloth make
good alternatives for tweed. Since the kilt is eminently acceptable for men there can be no reason why a lady should not also

wear one, or a skirt; for convenience in climbing on to transport and getting through fences, most prefer not to. A happy compromise, especially in warm weather, are culottes.

And so, on a fine morning in August we might find an attractively clad assortment of ladies going out with the Guns. One is in the same tweed as her husband, dark green with a brownish stripe, and has a divided skirt, and a corn-coloured tweed hat; another sports a man's cap, long, silky blonde hair, loden-cloth breeks, orange stockings and trainer shoes; a third wears smokey blue-grey cord knickerbockers and a dark pink cotton shirt, and one more appears in a green and brown check shirt and ruby-red corduroy breeches. Probably they will be told to keep down in the butt while birds are approaching, or don a drab-coloured waterproof, but the colours are a happy addition to the general cheerful atmosphere of the party.

At least the ladies no longer have to conform to the strict regime expected of those at shooting house-parties in the 1890s. Admittedly these were usually pheasant and partridge occasions in the south, but required raiment included a breakfast suit, tweeds for the shooting lunch and possibly a drive or two afterwards, a flamboyant tea gown and full evening dress for dinner. And with a different rig each day, naturally, a few days shooting might require fifteen or twenty outfits!

Some ladies shoot, as well as helping with the loading and keeping an eye on the dog. Most, however, are content to leave the actual gun wielding to the men. As one of them succinctly phrased it, 'If you do badly men despise you. If you shoot well they hate you.'

Among the accessories that people take to the grouse moor the most useful is a stick; and one for assistance in climbing up, and down, a steep hill is more useful than the shooting stick for sitting on. The best length climbing stick is one whose handle is just above the waist, not at shoulder height. Those long poles with a cunningly shaped and carved horn at the top are elegant to look at but not madly helpful for pushing yourself uphill; a thumb stick with the V up by your ear is really about 2 feet too long; keep it for a wading staff when salmon fishing, though admittedly a long stick can be useful for prodding ahead when coming down a very steep slope.

Another piece of equipment sometimes of extreme importance to one's well-being, if not survival, is a fly repellent. This is
to combat those midges mentioned in Chapter 2. You may
think this an unnecessary precaution, but it is a bit like carrying a
spare tyre in a car, or having foglamps fitted: most of the time
you never need them, but when you do, you really do! Incidentally, plastic squashable tubes of anti-midge cream are not
recommended since they are sure to be sat on sooner or later.

It is an odd fact, but entomologists tell us the female midge
insists on a meal from a mammal (Man, or Woman, will do) for
the successful maturation of its eggs. So if you forget your
anti-midge cream you may be offering a sacrifice for the benefit
of next year's midges, and thereby next year's grouse chicks,
which love to eat them.

A particular group of 'People' on the moor are the general
public, the walkers whose interests are to a certain extent
supported by the Ramblers' Association. This organization
wants 'public right of access on foot to all open country', its
aims deriving from a mass protest walk in 1932 by 400 hikers in
the Peak District of Derbyshire; they were objecting to being
barred from moorland which they thought was used by grouse
shooters for only a few days in the year. In 1949 the National
Parks and Access to the Countryside Act resulted in public
access being granted to certain areas; it also introduced procedures allowing public authorities to secure access to open
country by agreement, compulsory order or acquisition.

The Ramblers' Association claims that country walking is
'the most popular of the nation's outdoor recreations', although
as a participation sport ski-ing must run it close.

Highway authorities have a duty to signpost rights of way
where they leave roads. When such footpaths cross grouse
moors they need not cause interference with either the birds or
the shooting, assuming that walkers and their dogs keep to the
paths. Where they stray off the path and trespass on to nearby
property they can cause unnecessary harm, even if they do not
cause deliberate damage. Fortunately most country walkers
only want the exercise, the beautiful scenery and clean air; they
are not bent on causing mischief. Some shoots put up temporary
notices, 'Grouse Shooting in Progress,' to warn walkers, many

of whom in fact are quite interested to see what goes on, and are courteous enough not to interfere and to keep out of the way during a drive. Cases of mass trespass, however, occurred in 1982, when landowners were granted court injunctions to keep the offenders off grouse moors. One group of protestors did little to gain a reputation for accuracy, and much to alienate normal unprejudiced opinion, by issuing a leaflet which proclaimed:

'August 12th . . . is an important date in the social and sporting calendar of the rich, the Lords and the Colonels. Fitted in between Royal Ascot and Cowes Week on one side and the Henley Regatta on the other, it is the day when all come North and vie with each other to see who can bag the most grouse in a day of "glorious" carnage.' Apart from the somewhat rabble-rousing rhetoric, Ascot is mid-June, Cowes early August and Henley the end of June or early July.

Most landowners appreciate the wishes of today's mobile public to get out into the open countryside. Their main worry concerns the jealous vandal type who is apt to desecrate anything he believes others hold dear. Tolerance and mutual goodwill among all people who use the moor are needed: it should not be *quite* as difficult as the wolf dwelling with the lamb and the leopard lying down with the kid. . . .

4 The Keeper

'Ye're noo innit fer the monny,' he says, with much truth but no regrets. He has been on the estate for forty years and as well as looking after the grouse he has acted as ghillie to salmon-fishing guests, and often joined the deer-stalking parties. At least he knows that in retirement the estate will look after him with a rent-free cottage.

The keeper's job fills the whole year, and all hours of the day and night. He will be lucky if he ever receives the extra help he needs in times of special stress.

In the old days a beat keeper on a well-managed estate looked after about 3000 or 4000 acres of grouse moor. This was the figure recommended by the Committee of Enquiry into Grouse Disease, which published its report in 1911. The Committee also stated that three or four extra men should help the keeper with his heather burning. Nowadays a keeper may well have 10,000 acres to manage, and when it comes to assistance with heather burning he finds that the farm hands are busy with their own spring work, and men offered by the Job Centre are not fit enough.

The shortage of good men, and the economic difficulty of paying enough of them, gravely affects the success or otherwise of the modern grouse moor. Usually the big estate is more likely to succeed, being able to call on more staff to help each other in time of need. With a couple of low-ground keepers looking after the pheasants, a stalker or two and a river keeper, the moorland keeper, already with two assistants of his own, has a good chance of obtaining help when it is most needed. Smaller shoots are at a disadvantage.

The grouse's worst enemies are foxes and crows, and so control of these is one of the keeper's most important jobs, especially in springtime. A vixen with a growing family of cubs will take a lamb when she has the chance; this often occurs when twins are born and the ewe has difficulty in defending both the young at once. A much easier meal for the fox is a sitting grouse, when both bird and eggs will be eaten. Sometimes a vixen will carry the grouse chicks back to her earth to feed her own young, and a curious method of doing this has been observed. The chicks, about the size of sparrows, were ingeniously held together in a bunch of dried grass, the whole bundle being carried in a manner not unlike a gundog retrieving a practice dummy.

The keeper may use Cymag to gas foxes in their earth, or he may trap or snare their runs; or his terriers can drive out the inmates, which are then shot. He sometimes sits concealed, watching an earth, and shoots the fox when it emerges at dusk to hunt for food. In any case he is likely to spend many hours locating the earth in the first place and then dealing with its occupants. Cold, wet hours they often are, with dawn watches, on Sundays too, and no overtime pay.

These methods of fox killing are practised in the Highlands on territory unsuitable for foxhunting in the traditional way with hounds. In the south the local hunt will control foxes but the keeper will also have his own ways of dealing with those in inaccessible places.

The spring fox is the real villain the keeper has to contend with. Throughout the year the animal kills to eat, that is Nature's way; at this time it wipes out whole families of grouse. When the chicks appear the fox will eat the lot, ignoring any broken-wing trick by the mother in her frantic attempts to draw him away from her nestlings hiding in the heather.

By killing hen grouse while they are brooding, foxes not only remove that covey from the subsequent August scene but also create a number of surplus widower cocks. If there are not enough hens to go round at the autumn pairing the extra cocks band together and can give a false impression of a better mixed stock on the ground than is truly the case. This effect can be cumulative over the years if fox control is neglected.

Tom Speedy, an experienced and observant nineteenth-century gamekeeper, wrote of a unique fox-catching episode by a keeper friend of his on the Atholl estate in Perthshire. This man one day spied a fox asleep in the heather below the hill where he stood. Used to stalking deer, the keeper moved round to get downwind of the fox, and cautiously approached it. At about 30 yards he raised his gun, and then decided against shooting; instead he would see just how close he could get to this normally wary animal. Slowly he advanced until he was standing over the fox. He bent down; it must have heard his breathing for it woke up and he was staring straight into its eyes. It seemed momentarily paralysed and he quickly pressed the barrels of his gun across its neck, half throttling it.

This canny Scot then grabbed the fox by the back of the neck and shoved its body between his knees (he wearing the kilt!). He took a piece of string from his pocket, muzzled the fox, and carried it home in his game-bag to show his children; a story probably 'unprecedented in the annals of the sportsman or foxhunter'. Who wouldn't agree, particularly the foxhunter!

Carrion crows, and their northern counterparts the hooded crows, are the next to claim the keeper's urgent attention. They steal eggs and kill chicks up to six weeks old. They can be caught in large wire-netting cage traps, like a box some 12 feet each way, with a funnel entrance in the roof. Crows are very wary birds, however, and not so liable to be caught like this as the less damaging jackdaws, rooks, magpies and jays.

The keeper shoots crows, ambushing them as they return to their nests; he also destroys the nests whenever he can, and in this way is always alerted when he sees a new one in the spring.

Stoats and weasels are trapped, usually with a Fenn trap. The weasel, incidentally, if you are doubtful about identification, is the smaller of the two; the stoat also has a longer tail with a black tag on the end, well known as a prime ingredient of the Stoat's Tail salmon fly. These little animals are comparatively rare on a grouse moor although they do occur on the lower ground. They are both egg stealers and will sometimes kill chicks and even adults.

Black-backed gulls also steal eggs and are a prime target for the keeper's gun. The domestic cat which has reverted to the

The keeper checks a fox earth with his terriers. They will soon tell him if anyone s at home

The keeper inspects a trap This is a Fenn trap, placed in a tunnel artificially formed of stones. One top slab has been removed, revealing a stoat caught in the trap

wild is another enemy to watch; it can do immense harm over a fairly small area since it kills for fun and not just for food. An old though rather cruel remedy to prevent domestic cats going hunting was to crop their ears; it was thought that cats could not bear rain or dew getting into so sensitive an organ. The true wild cat is sufficiently rare to be little trouble. A newcomer to the vermin list is the mink. Originally escaped from fur farms, these animals have now spread to many parts of the country, usually staying near rivers; but on some lower moors, up to about 500 feet, they form one more problem, especially since they also kill more than they require as food.

Birds of prey may not be shot: the Protection of Birds Acts 1954 and 1967 protect all birds, other than game, and then list those which may be killed. These lists do not include hen harrier, buzzard, sparrowhawk, owl, etc.

The good gamekeeper does not use poison. Unfortunately, he becomes liable to blame and unfair criticism through the action of a small minority of farmers and the occasional rogue gamekeeper. Every year poisoning incidents are reported to the Royal Society for the Protection of Birds, and doubtless others go undetected. The baits are rabbit or sheep carcasses and hens' eggs, and the object is to kill foxes and crows; but victims include golden eagles, red kites, sparrowhawks, buzzards, marsh harriers and dogs and cats. Strychnine, the insecticide mevinphos and the narcotic alphachloralose are all used by unscrupulous miscreants who thereby tend to bring the shooting community into disrepute; in fact, by helping to stamp out illegal poisoning, the shooting community assists in the preservation of wildlife.

Vermin control is a continuous task for the keeper, especially in the spring when his charges are most vulnerable. When neighbouring moorland is ploughed up and re-afforested he views the proceedings with a jaundiced eye: as the trees grow they will form a first class sanctuary for vermin. His traps and snares must be visited daily, and that task alone takes up a considerable part of his time. Sometimes, when his land is crossed by public roads or footpaths – and certain walks, like the Pennine Way, the Southern Uplands Way, and Coast to Coast, do cross many grouse moors – he is troubled by over zealous do-gooders who spring his traps, or even steal them, in the belief that they are saving some oppressed animal.

Poachers are less of a problem on the moor than on a lowland pheasant shoot, although the man with a .22 rifle, shooting from a car, can cause damage, particularly among paired birds in the spring. Ordinary human disturbance does not worry the grouse as much as might be expected, but out-of-control dogs can scatter the young coveys, which may suffer in windy and wet weather. Poachers on the low ground amongst the woodland will always take a certain number of pheasants: one keeper was particularly saddened when he and his colleague from the hill caught a gang of three men with forty pheasants; the leader was fined £9 and the other two £5 each, but the disgruntled keeper had to pay £18 because his Alsatian had torn the trousers of one of them. It seems that magistrates sometimes fail to support gamekeepers adequately, and to punish the offence of poaching for what it is – stealing.

Sufficient punishment or not, keepers are unanimous in insisting that an apprehended poacher must be prosecuted. Letting them off with a caution never pays. 'They just think you're soft if you do, and they'll be there again almost as soon as your back's turned!'

There is one curious poacher's trick that is mentioned by several of the old writers, though all of them were doubtful of its efficacy – and doubtful about the length to which their legs were being pulled! It is the one using a champagne bottle. The poacher has to be a local man who knows the areas frequented by grouse; after a heavy snowfall he goes to one of these before dusk and makes some deep indentations with his bottle, neck downwards. Then he sprinkles corn all around, with some in the bottom of the hole. The night's frost hardens the snow, the birds come along to eat the corn and presently discover that all that remains is in the holes. So they eagerly stretch down for this, as far as they can possibly reach, and plop! They tumble in. The champagne bottle size is just a nice fit for their bodies and the barb effect of rearward facing feathers prevents any upward movement, however hard they may wriggle and scrabble with their feet. A supremely simple plan, with the birds just waiting for the poacher to come along and pick them up! One wonders who started the idea and whether any bird has ever been caught that way. The brilliant artist and zoologist J. G. Millais, wrote that both his mother and an old poacher told him this trick, and he even drew a picture of the arrangement, complete with upended bird. He was the son of Sir John Millais and father of Raoul, one of today's most distinguished painters.

Another one-time form of poaching was known in the north of England as grouse becking. The word 'beck' derives from that part of the grouse's vocabulary when he stands on a knoll, rock, tussock or whatever prominence is handy and declares that territory his own; different authorities describe the call as including sounds such as 'eck, kek, beck, wuk, go-back, go-back'. The bird intersperses the call with jumping flights several feet into the air.

The hunter would go out to the moor before dawn and conceal himself, probably behind a wall; as the light came and the cock grouse called, the man called too, as another challenging male or as an enticing hen. The decoy call might be a purely vocal effort, or aided by some contrivance such as a hollowed stick or the stem of a clay pipe. Either way, when it was sufficient to entice the inquisitive grouse, he paid the penalty. The best 'season' for this activity is autumn, when the birds are pairing and the pugnacious attitude of the cocks so easily leads them into trouble. But who nowadays can raise an effective decoy call? The keeper will know, even if he does not talk about it.

Grouse were sometimes taken by netting them on the ground at night, and by putting up nets slung between posts and allowing the birds to fly into them by day. This sort of poaching might be done in order to kill the birds and sell them to game dealers, or to take them alive and offer them to other estates who were trying to increase their stock.

Nobody has sympathy for the commercial poacher but there lingers a certain modicum of admiration for the countryman who has a little scheme to help himself to the fruits of the earth, and maybe the fowls of the air as well.

One such scheme involved grouse, and blackgame, feeding on the cornfields after the harvest. In the days when stooks were left around the fields it was a common sight to see both red grouse and black sitting on top of them gobbling up the grain; often the tenant farmers complained. When most, or better still, all the stooks had been taken in for threshing the artful schemer collected a few sheaves and built himself his own stook, with a stake in the middle to help hold them up. At the top he fixed a short cross-piece, handy for perching, and if he was a skilful and conscientious operator he had a stuffed decoy bird on the perch. Hiding inside his stook he waited for customers; when they arrived he gently poked his hand through the top and grabbed them by the legs! Some of these poaching stories are, of course, difficult to test, but they do make wonderful collector's pieces.

Butt building and repair is a summer job, in which the keeper shows his skill and ingenuity. (Some of the different types of butt were mentioned in Chapter 1.) Building the dry-stone type, more often seen in England than Scotland, takes time. As in any wall building, there has to be a foundation, and the first course of stones is placed below ground level. Even then a dry summer, during which the surrounding peat contracts, can cause a minor subsidence and a leaning wall. Once built, however, dry stone butts are the most robust and are practically sheep proof.

In rocky areas butts are sometimes built making use of an existing rock of the right size and in the right place. Occasionally a convenient ravine may eliminate the need for butts at all, the Guns merely standing by numbered sticks, as at a pheasant shoot. Better still, a wall crossing the hill in the right place provides excellent ready-made cover for the Guns to stand behind. Even then the ground where the Guns will actually stand should be made firm and level.

Butts also need numbering, and it is the keeper who must ensure that this is done, usually by painting white numbers on them.

During a drive when the birds are coming briskly there is hectic activity in a butt; when a loader is being used there are two men moving around, sometimes facing the front, sometimes the rear. Perhaps a wife or other spectator is present, and also a dog – although a better place for the latter is outside. The butt, therefore, must be big enough, with an inside width of not less

Shooting from behind a wall When it is in the right place the wall obviates the need to build butts

Surprise! An unusual sight in the viewfinder; all stations go!

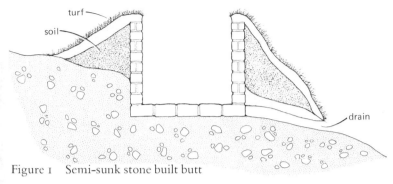

Figure 1 Semi-sunk stone built butt

than 4 feet – 5 or 6 feet is better. A good height inside is 4 feet 6 inches.

For added safety it is preferable for butts to be square rather than round. In the heat of the moment during a bird-filled drive, it is possible for the shooter in a round butt to become slightly confused as to where precisely is his front. He could then take a shot, imagining it to be safe, when in fact it is down the line of butts and endangering his neighbour. A great number of fine old butts, particularly in the north of England, are round and cannot be condemned for that. Nonetheless the square shape can be safer. Butts designed to face only one way have a straight front in any case, so confusion about direction hardly arises, unless the front is not parallel to the line of butts. Similarly, H-shaped double-drive butts must be square to the front.

The Rolls-Royce type of butt is stone-built and semi-sunk, the stone-flagged floor being 18 inches or so below ground level. It is drained by a pipe leading underground until the slope of the ground brings it to the surface. The sides of the butt are sloped, with soil topped by turf or heather, making it almost unnoticeable from the front (see Figure 1).

Good moor management is almost a catch phrase as far as grouse shooting is concerned. With it you have a good chance of turning a reasonable piece of grouse habitat into a successful shoot; without it you have not. With many patches of young heather available grouse territories for a pair of birds can be as little as four or five acres, which means a high stock on the moor. When much of the heather is old and the nutritious young growth is scarce, territories become much bigger, and the stock diminishes. The keeper's most important jobs, therefore, are to burn the heather, in order to encourage new growth to provide food for the birds, and then to assess the stock before shooting begins, so that adequate bags may be made. It is quite a responsibility.

Heather burning, often known as 'muir burn' in Scotland, is by no means indiscriminate: it is done in strips and carefully controlled. A distant view of a well-burnt hill reveals a chequer-board of light and dark patches 300 or 400 yards long, perhaps nearly a mile, but only about 30 yards wide. The aim, rarely achieved, is to work round the whole area in twelve to fifteen years, depending on the rate of re-growth, which itself is dependent on a dry climate and fertile soil.

Legally, burning may begin in Scotland in October but it may not continue after mid-April; in England and Wales the season is 1 November to 31 March with an extension in Northumberland and Durham to 15 April. In most years very little can be done during winter because the ground is too wet and often, even in April, snow still lies on high moors. On many estates autumn and early winter burning is also restricted because the staff are occupied with deer stalking and pheasant shooting.

Fires are usually lit with a paraffin torch, and controlled by beating with a metal besom; normally a team of two or three is sufficient for one fire but if the ground is exceptionally dry seven or eight men may be required. Huge areas of blackened, devastated terrain must be avoided.

The modern type of besom, or scraper, is rectangular, with the longer side parallel to its handle. Wire netting is fixed to the frame and this shape enables the user to follow up behind the edges of the fire strip, beating and scrubbing at the burning heather to prevent it spreading outward. Another useful adaptation to the normal long tube handle is to have the front third of aluminium and the other two-thirds iron; when held about the middle this gives a better balance and is less tiring. The principle is similar to that of having a fishing reel of the correct weight to balance its rod.

Long, narrow fires are the best because the unburnt areas between such strips give cover for the grouse to nest. As the chicks will not normally stray further than 20 yards from heather tall enough to provide cover, a burnt patch, and the resultant new growth, should be available close to the nest.

Wind has very great effect on the fires, far more than inexperienced people might realize. Even quite damp heather will burn if there is a good wind. The keeper uses the wind and the lie of the land to help him control his fire; for instance, by directing it into a hollow, out of the wind, he can more easily put it out. Strong winds can be best, provided there is a fire break in front, because the fire can then be kept narrow, whereas a light wind will usually mean that the fire will fan out wider and wider. A changeable wind, continually altering direction, precludes burning altogether.

The standard way of controlling all fires, whether in war-stricken cities or raging, flaming forests, is to have a fire break, a burnt line which the approaching fire cannot cross, because nothing combustible remains there.

When a heather fire is very hot, with long, old, dry material flaring up strongly, the team can tire easily, for it is then much harder work. Care must be taken about wearing protective clothing – too much can lull the wearer into a false sense of security so that he scorches himself. A perspex visor is essential, although it is not worn in the down position all the time, and leather gauntlets are often needed.

Looking ahead to the following season, the heather burner has an eye to his fire breaks, burning along the boundary, along the top of a ridge, or close to a sheep fence. If this is carefully done when conditions are right there will be less anxiety the following year when conditions may be more difficult. A raging fire by a wire fence can burn the posts or melt the wire but if a keeper can achieve a fire break along the top of a ridge it will be a useful bonus. A fire break may be a road or stream or even a grassy area.

Burning over peat is particularly hazardous, especially where it has been exposed after drainage trenches have been dug. 'I was sitting down once eating my sandwiches,' the keeper says. 'Suddenly the heather about half a mile away burst into flame. The peat must have been smouldering away without any smoke for days. I always carry a can in the Land-Rover and I drove across, got some water from a drain and put out the fire.'

Sometimes water to quench a fire has to be carried in back-packs borrowed from the Forestry Commission or the estate for-esters.

Proper control of a fire is achieved only with experience and by a man with an eye for country. The fire must not be too hot, or it will burn the seeds in the earth; nor must it just blacken the top of the heather, scarcely touching the bottom, as it will if the ground is too wet. On a long steep hill a fire started at the bottom may easily fan out and be beyond control by the time it reaches the top. The correct drill is to start some way down from the top of the hill, let the fire burn up, extinguish it, and then go downhill and burn up another patch to meet the first.

There are plenty of problems for the keeper to think about in his plans for heather burning. Somehow he has to preserve plenty of young heather shoots at the right height, 4 or 5 inches. If they are higher the chicks cannot reach them, and if too many sheep are in the area they will graze the shoots down almost to nothing. An additional function of burning may be to clear a strip in front of a line of butts, so that the birds do not land there during a drive; a similar burnt area behind the butts helps in picking up, but these extras have a low priority in the burning programme.

Heather burning must be regarded as of over-riding import-ance because there are so few days when conditions are suitable, and on these occasions staff should be allowed to drop every-thing in order to burn. Some estates provide board and lodging for parties of students at the end of March. These young men can work on roads, drains and butts during wet weather, and be immediately diverted by the keeper on to burning as soon as conditions permit. Even if they sit around idle some of the time their wages will not be wasted if at least *some* good burning is achieved.

Although a neglected moor needs a considerable gang to complete enough burning to bring it into shape, a properly burnt one can be maintained by a single keeper plus three or four men at burning times, though the maximum area he could deal with would be about 8000 acres.

An experienced eye can quickly assess the efficiency of the burning on any moor, and at the same time judge the standard of the management of the whole shoot. Avoiding disasters, and given reasonable general conditions, a keeper should aim at having in May a pair of grouse to about every five acres, each pair's territory containing both tall and short heather.

Some keepers are loath to burn in the autumn because they think the heather is slower in regenerating than when it is burnt in the spring. This is a mistaken belief, and with the shortage of days suitable for burning, perhaps only about twenty, advantage should be taken of any dry spell in the early winter; this particularly applies to north-facing slopes which may still be covered with snow in the spring.

Annual heather burning is often planned haphazardly, with the result that many moors have a smaller stock of grouse than they *could* support. It is so important that although the keeper will actually do most of it, the overall control should be in the hands of the estate factor or manager, or owner; the recording of areas burnt, and the planning of future areas to be burnt, should be marked on a map. If an exceptionally good burning year occurs every advantage should be taken of it, even after the planned target has been reached. No moor is ever burnt as much as it should be, and a little extra one year will help to make up for other wet autumns and snow-laden springs.

If the object of burning is to provide food for the birds another task for the keeper is to see that they can always get at it, particularly after a heavy snowfall with little wind. A blizzard creates deep drifts of snow but it also leaves other slopes comparatively bare, with the heather scarcely covered. A heavy blanket of snow in quiet conditions buries all the heather, and the grouse may starve or depart for a more hospitable neighbourhood. Then is the time when the keepers must be out to rake the snow away from a few patches of heather. If they are lucky they may be helped by sheep, cattle or deer trampling the snow as they search for grazing themselves.

Because so many grouse die anyway from natural causes before they are twenty months old, the shooting policy needs to be varied according to the breeding success of the year. About half of the birds on the ground in August will die during the winter, less if it has been a good breeding season with four or more young birds per pair; this should mean some increase in stock the following spring, and a reasonable bag to aim at would be about a third of the August stock.

In a poor breeding year with two or less young per pair the object should be to shoot about half the August stock. This is the crunch, because owners are inclined to think that after poor breeding they should shoot lightly and 'leave a good stock for next year'. But most of the birds they spare will die during the winter anyway. A restrictive shooting policy is called for when a small stock breeds well and so a bigger stock for breeding next spring may be expected. In nearly all other cases shooting stops with the moor still holding a surplus of birds, which could have been shot if the owner had known what his stock was at the beginning of the season.

Therefore, the grouse have to be counted, although keepers have always been reluctant to say on 11 August how many birds will appear next day! Dogs are used to find the birds before the season starts, and one method is to choose several areas of a couple of hundred acres, walk them carefully up and down and count the birds as they are flushed. Knowing the number of areas and the total acreage of the beat you can form quite a good estimate of total numbers, and so at least make a plan for shooting that beat. Admittedly, when this sort of counting is done by some advisory body the reaction of the keeper is apt to be, 'By –, what a waste o' bloomin' time. He only counted 'em in little small patches.'

The keeper should, of course, count his pairs in the spring, and with the help of a dog he can count the chicks in several sample broods in July, including nought chicks for barren pairs. This should give a reasonable prediction of the average size of coveys in August.

The Spring count, over the same areas each year, and probably carried out in March before the birds become aggressive, should yield a figure for the Grouse Breeding Stock. This can be in terms of a hen per so many acres. The count should not be done after late snow or floods at hatching time which can upset the figure.

In the July count the keeper should walk the drives with his dogs right up to the butts, checking numbers, and do the same back again to the start line. The total number of birds counted in this way forms a very good estimate of the season's bag in *brace*. It is a vital figure in planning the shooting programme, but it does assume a fairly high standard of marksmanship by the Guns.

Because of the importance and usefulness of counting the birds before the season starts, a detailed explanation of how it can be done appears in Appendix F. The system is described by Mr Kenneth Wilson, for many years head keeper at Leadhills, Lanarkshire.

One way a keeper can estimate the number of nesting hens is by observing their droppings. In the ordinary way a grouse walking about and feeding excretes brownish cylinders of fibrous matter about 1 inch long; these are a common sight all over the moor. When brooding, the hen stays on the nest as much as possible, coming off twice a day to feed and drink and then she drops a much bigger lump of ordure about 3 inches long and coloured green when fresh; these are usually found near water and when the keeper sees them, from his experience of previous years he will be able to judge how many hens have nests. These droppings, conspicuous when you know where to look, are found only in the nesting season and are sometimes called 'clocker' droppings, or 'clocker's' droppings, referring to the sitting hen as a clocker. This curious word derives from cloaca, which is a bird's excretory cavity.

So, we might list the how-many-do-we-shoot part of the keeper's duties like this:

1 Find out numbers of birds on the ground by July.
2 Determine what stock can survive the winter, bearing in mind unpredictable problems such as the severity of the winter and whether the birds will migrate.
3 If it is a good season, plan to shoot hard, early.
4 If it is a poor season, shoot lightly, and mostly the old birds.
5 Regulate the stock by the numbers to remain, not the bags to be obtained. It probably needs a clairvoyant Solomon to achieve this, and doubtless the owner will have his views, too.

This is the theory of it but pundits pontificating is not the same as the actual practical experiences of the man on the ground. He may be inclined to say, 'What about that snow in February and March? Couldn't do *any* heather burning this year.'

Or, 'We had snow in April (or June). Lost a lot of young birds.'

And, 'There's ticks everywhere, birds dying all over the place, Guv'nor says we won't start till September, and then only do a few days.'

The moor keeper's lot is a busy one, and a great deal more complicated than that of his colleague looking after a pheasant shoot. Grouse, the wild bird, not *quite* unpredictable, is beset with a multitude of awkward characteristics, and the keeper who is less than first class may be more inclined to make excuses than predictions.

Bracken is another problem for the keeper. Heather takes a few years to regenerate while bracken grows fast; furthermore, its rhizomes are deep in the ground and escape damage by fire. Since it also grows much taller than heather it can form a canopy beneath which the heather suffers and finally is extinguished.

Bracken can be cut or sprayed with special weedkiller, as mentioned in Chapter 1. Helicopter spraying is effective but expensive, about £45 an acre in 1986. The eventual result is to do away with the mat of old bracken and grass which makes ideal conditions for ticks which carry louping ill. Instead of rubbish the hill should soon be supporting heather and bilberry again. The expenses of removing bracken can be offset by a grant, although this may be dependent on an undertaking to fertilize the ground afterwards to improve the grazing.

Care is needed when the keeper is burning his heather not to burn right up to a patch of bracken, because this makes it easier for the bracken to spread out into the place where the heather was. It is better to stop the fire short, leaving a strip of old heather to deter the advance of the bracken.

When bracken has been eradicated the area may be grazed by sheep, and the keeper will have strong ideas of a suitable stocking rate: something like one ewe to three acres. Light grazing on the new heather is good, like pruning in the garden: remove the top shoots to encourage lateral growth.

Grazing needs controlling, however. If it is too concentrated sheep will nibble the young heather to the ground and even pull up the very small plants. Heavy grazing by too many animals reduces the height of the older heather so that there is insufficient cover for grouse; and when the birds do not like their habitat they move elsewhere.

The keeper would like to have the ultimate say in rulings about grazing but this is virtually impossible because of agreements with the tenants. And in the north of England the stint system still operates.

Grazing rights are a complex subject with different rules in different places. There may be tied flocks, sometimes called hefts, where the sheep belong to the land and remain on it even in a change of tenancy. Or the farmer may just rent the land and please himself about how he grazes it. Or stints may be allocated, these being rights of individuals to graze a certain number of sheep on the moor. Whatever the rules they often permit access by too many sheep.

Many stint holders on a comparatively small acreage means a great deal of movement by men and dogs over the moor, all potentially disturbing to the grouse and quite likely causing loss of nests and eggs. This can be aggravated when sheep are driven to the fanks or pens for the castration of the lambs, and later for dipping and for shearing.

Sheep can be a terrible headache for the keeper; if their owners fail to have them regularly dosed for worms and dipped for ticks he is in trouble. If the graziers, farmers and shepherds run unruly dogs he will lose young grouse; if they decide to do a bit of off-hand burning he may have a runaway fire to deal with, losing in the process good heather and possibly birds as well.

But, of course, usually the shepherd is the keeper's ally, a source of invaluable intelligence about vermin, poachers, strangers and untoward happenings generally. Incidentally, the breeds of sheep most likely to be met on a grouse moor are the Black-faced and the Cheviot. The former is reckoned to be hardier and to be prepared to eat older and tougher heather; it is commonly found in the Highlands. The Cheviot tends to require better and grassier land and is the type usually seen in Northumberland or Yorkshire.

Heather burning The keeper in charge watches his fire; he wears a visor and carries a metal besom for bumping out the fire at its edges

Over grazing The wall down the centre divides an area to the right where grazing is controlled, heather flourishes, and grouse abound. To the left the land is grazed almost bare and no grouse live there at all

Sheep do give some small benefits by forming paths through the deep heather, by scooping out hollows in south-facing banks where the birds can dust themselves and by turning up a certain amount of grit. And their droppings are favourite breeding spots for insects, a food source for grouse chicks. But in excessive numbers they may cause an extra expense to the landowner, who has to put up fencing round newly burnt ground to protect the tender young heather for a few years.

A sidelight on the importance of sheep as an influence on moor management is their considerably increased value in recent years; from this arises the need to have some restriction on numbers in the tenant's agreement. Furthermore, there is a greater incentive for the farmer to feed his sheep, particularly in winter, and not merely accept the fact that in hard weather some animals will starve, as was the case in the old days. 'Foddering', that is, feeding with hay, is forbidden in some areas, as is supplying extra nutrition in the form of synthetic foods like Rumevite. Where this is allowed a less efficient farmer is inclined to dump the blocks of Rumevite in the same place each time, which results in a deterioration of the surrounding heather to the point where only grass is left. And rarely does he pick up the containers, leaving a glut of plastic bags to litter the countryside. It can be a cause of friction between owner and tenant.

A long, cold winter causes 'frosting' of the heather, which turns it brown. This means less food heather in the spring and consequently a smaller hatch; and in the autumn each pair of birds requires a bigger territory. If the heather is not frosted there should be plenty of it in the autumn to accommodate more grouse territories. Frosting, or browning, is familiar to the keeper; he knows that this colour can sometimes be caused by drought or scorching by fire. But another influence may also be at work: it is called the heather beetle *(Lochmaea suturalis)*.

This creature, about ¼ inch long, emerges from hibernation in the spring, flies around for a while and then lays its eggs in sphagnum moss; it likes a nice damp place. The grubs climb nearby heather stems and eat the leaves and young shoots, and by July the damage is apparent in the rusty red colour of the heather and the chewed appearance of the shoots. The grubs later spend about a month in the soil, emerge as adults around

September, when the year-old adults die, leaving the new crop of beetles to hibernate by November.

The affected heather turns a pale grey the following year and finally withers and dies. There is not much the keeper can do about the heather beetle except look to his drainage, which is part of good moor management anyway. He might sometimes be able to break up some moss patches if he can get a tractor and harrow to it. Burning does not affect the hibernators deep in the ground, and chemical control is scarcely practicable owing to the risk to grouse in the heather. Fortunately, the grubs are preyed on by two different parasites and by the ladybird beetle, so it has to be left to Nature to redress the balance after an abundance of heather beetles.

Draining the moor improves the quality of the heather and the grass. Crossleaved heath, or bell heather *(Erica cinerea)* sometimes grows on damp ground and is not much use to grouse, which eat only its flowers. Drain the ground and you will encourage the much more useful and palatable ling heather. In Chapter 1 open drains leading diagonally down the hill were described as a recognizable feature of a cared-for moor, rather than a neglected piece of wild land. But these open drains can be dangerous to young birds in times of flood and may cause erosion in the gullies they flow into. Coupled with draining is the job of ensuring that the birds have sufficient water to drink; this can be done by opening up springs and allowing small pools to form.

On some moors there is an impervious layer beneath the peat which is bound to become waterlogged after heavy rain. If the peat is not more than about 2 feet deep the hard subsoil can be broken with a subsoiler plough, and then the water in the peat can drain away vertically. This is an expensive job, but with the shortage and high cost of labour any such tasks that can be done mechanically are worthwhile, and agricultural grants for hill drainage are available. Since rearing grouse like pheasants is impossible, the main theme of the keeper's responsibility is to improve their environment.

Providing a good supply of grit is another way of helping the birds, particularly if it can be placed near their nesting areas. This reduces the time the hen bird has to spend off her nest searching for it, time when her eggs are exposed to predators; it also lessens the need for any of the birds to seek their grit from road chippings, where they are easily seen by two-legged intruders, who may feel disposed to bring a gun along early one morning. Grit is often placed near butts so that birds visiting it become used to seeing them at close hand.

The keeper whose moor is devoid of much natural grit will have to buy it, and the price will vary according to how far it has to be brought. If there is no quarry nearby he might have to pay £80 a ton and use half a ton a year, while an estate in a very peaty area could use as much as 7 tons a year. First class quartz grit is imported from Norway. Some also comes from Cornwall. Grit is always welcome and if you put it out you will surely find some later in the gizzards of the birds you shoot.

After all the months of preparation, as the shooting season draws near, the keeper and the owner, or tenant, make their plans. They may decide to have some walking-up days first before driving begins. This does not involve much complicated organization on the part of the keeper: a few assistants to carry the game and some dog men with retrievers to find it after it has been shot. Perhaps the party will be going 'dogging', which means the use of pointers or setters to find the birds; arrangements can probably be made with the staff of the estate. But when it is to be a driving day a great deal more organization is required by the keeper, beginning with the beaters.

As many as thirty beaters will be needed early in the season, especially in hot weather when birds tend to sit tight. Later on, when the grouse are wilder, half that number can suffice. If the shoot can afford the cost, two lines of beaters may be recruited, on top of which the keeper has to find flankers and pickers-up. Two lines are particularly useful when return drives are operated, the first lot, having done a drive, going to the next start line while the second party carries out its drive.

Normal procedure in the beating line is to have the head keeper in the middle, with a distinctively coloured flag, probably red, and the beaters forming a crescent curving forward to each side, an assistant keeper or other responsible man at each end. The length of the line might be half a mile and the distance from the start to the butts perhaps a mile, or in certain circumstances up to three miles; too long a drive only results in birds flying out to the side, despite the efforts of the flankers.

These key men take up position in front of the butts and to the side, and should lie down and watch, very attentively. As the keeper brings his men forward birds will rise and fly towards, although not necessarily as far as, the butts; if they tend to veer off to one side the flankers there leap into action, waving their flags; their sudden appearance is often enough to turn the birds back towards the butts. Determined grouse, however, flying directly at right angles to a line of flag wavers, are unlikely to be put off their objective.

If possible there should be several flankers, not just one old retired shepherd and the keeper's wife, who may themselves be perfectly capable but are insufficient for the job. Flankers should be experienced people and able to use their initiative, so that they move their position during the drive if necessary. It is the keeper's responsibility to select sensible flankers and to see that they are properly briefed. To be really effective they need to be 30 yards or so apart, closer when guarding a leeward flank in a cross wind; this is rarely achieved, however, because of the shortage and expense of staff.

Good flankers can save a drive. If their initial efforts are apparently ignored they should run towards the birds, an action often surprisingly effective! One flanker at each end of the butts armed with a whistle can be a great help to Guns behind a crest or in a gully, by giving warning as birds approach.

A flanker close to the butts must make sure he is seen by the Guns, before and during the drive; flankers further out remain concealed until birds approach them. Then they get up and wave. It is particularly important not to start flag waving when grouse are flying well to the butts, because this may scare them away out of the drive, to the chagrin of the Guns – 'That dam' fool flanker scared off a fine lot of birds that were coming straight to me!' It is the keeper who gets the blame.

Beaters, too, need briefing by the keeper, especially the inexperienced ones. Their job is not just to walk across country to the butts but to scare into flight birds which may be partially tame, in as much as they have seen humans walk over the moor before; hence 'Keep those flags going!' he admonishes, over the

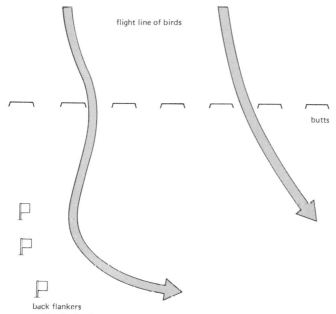

flight line of birds

butts

back flankers

Figure 2   Back flankers

roughest scrambly kind of terrain and right up to the end of the drive.

One extra piece of technique concerns back flanking, which means turning the birds *after* they have passed the butts. The object of this is to direct birds into the area of the next drive rather than allow them to escape out of the field of operations. It is a logical idea, but again increases the number of paid assistants to the day's sport. Figure 2 shows some of these back flankers, well behind the butts, persuading any recalcitrant fliers to join the main throng navigating as the keeper intended.

In making the shooting plan the great difficulty is to keep it flexible. For best results, and with a big enough acreage, the days on which different beats are to be shot should not be fixed in advance; the weather may force changes. Furthermore, the birds must not be harassed too much, or they may go. And when they come back there may be too many of them, with the consequent increase of disease. After shooting four days a week for two weeks it is advisable to rest the moor for the next week; advice that some owners may be reluctant to take.

The keeper will have conferred with his boss before the plan for the day is formed, but even then changes may have to be made when they get out on to the ground. Wind is a main deciding factor; if it is in the wrong direction when the beaters are all deployed it may be necessary to divert the Guns to a different line of butts.

The principles on which the keeper works out the drives are:

1 He starts with a drive down wind.
2 Each drive should as far as possible feed birds in to the next one.
3 He takes an upwind drive after a downwind one. Birds are then less reluctant to go against the wind because they are going towards their home ground.
4 He hopes he will not have to wait too long for this return drive, otherwise the birds will start moving back too soon. For example, if lunchtime intervenes the keeper bites his nails while the Guns savour steak and kidney pie and claret.
5 The crescent shape of the line of beaters may be exaggerated to become almost a horseshoe shape.
6 The beaters do not necessarily start parallel to the butts and walk towards them. Sometimes, owing to the particular nature of the ground, disturbed grouse will fly in a curve, even completing most of a circle to arrive eventually in their original area. The beaters may thus start walking at right angles to the butts, or even almost directly away from them for a short way. (See Figure 3)
7 In a cross wind, while himself remaining in the centre of the drive, the keeper will deploy more beaters on the downwind end of the line, which itself will be further forward than the middle of the crescent. (See Figure 4)
8 Birds are driven to a known natural settling area, not just to the butts; these should have been sited to intercept the usual flight lines.

Some schemes for deciding on the siting of butts and the direction of drives may be worked out by keeper and owner together by experiments on the ground on non-shooting days. Driving grouse is an art, and beautiful to watch, like hunting hounds or casting to a salmon. As an example of the reactions of

Grouse fly to X, to Y and then over the butts

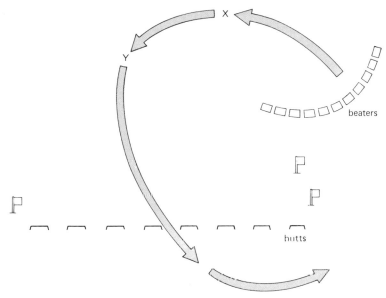

Figure 3   Beaters initially going away from butts

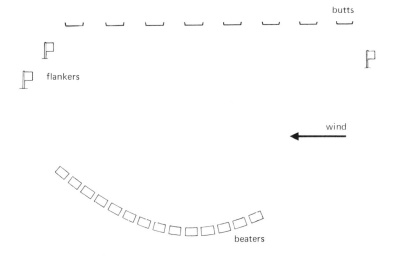

Figure 4   Driving with a cross wind

a well-trained team of beaters, consider the situation of the start of a drive with the wind blowing towards the nearby march. A crest allows the leeward beaters to start advancing out of sight of a known holding area for birds. As the drive begins several birds some way ahead get up, mildly alarmed but not yet setting a course for distant places. Immediately the windward beaters lie down. The birds circle and settle, not too worried after all. When the drive continues the leeward beaters are in place to persuade forward, in the direction of the butts, birds which, facing a less well drilled beating line, would have been over the march and away. Too fanciful with modern beater material? It is nevertheless a standard of understanding aimed at on the best estates.

When the wind is strong the grouse often go for shelter into gullies, and are difficult to drive. They also fail to oblige by following their usual flight lines, and so the keeper may have to discard his normal butts and place the Guns in other gullies, keeping the drives quite short. In a really strong wind, whipping up to a gale, the day may have to be cancelled.

Another upset to the best laid plans is mist or fog on the high hills. This often necessitates a complete change of plan, probably moving down to a lower beat. Some shoots employ walkie-talkie radios for communication in such cases between keeper and guv'nor. These radios can also be invaluable in calling for assistance in case of accidents or an intrusion by poachers.

In bad visibility the keeper has an extra responsibility in getting his charges off the hill, especially the youngsters and visitors who do not know their way around the area. Some of these can be more than a little irresponsible. A keeper who brought his party off the hill in nasty conditions of rain and mist found that two of the lads were missing. No one knew where they could be and a laborious search was made by the keepers and estate workers, without success. One under-keeper, leading the rest of the party down a track to return to the transport, came upon the two bedraggled boys who, when asked what they thought they were doing, replied, 'We got wet so we thought we'd just go 'ome. Which way is it?'

One of the disadvantages of taking out young beaters, especially when they come from the local villages, is that they are apt to come inadequately dressed for a sudden change in the weather. Then the keeper gets into trouble from their irate mothers when they return home in a terrible state!

Another unexpected problem with the boys is that they may have to be off the hill to play in the school or village football match. Says the keeper, 'They never tell yer when y' study books on keeperin' how to get yer beaters to the football!' Generally the keeper welcomes youngsters because while their school holidays last it is easy to find sufficient beaters. And, as he says, 'The smaller they are the more you can pack into the Land-Rover!'

In the absence of the owner of the moor, the keeper may have trouble with the paying guests who want another drive at 4.30 in the afternoon. He knows what the bag should be for the day, and which ground covered, and he also knows that many of the staff have a long way to go to get home. The low-ground keepers have their own chores to attend to as well, like feeding their pheasants, and this is an argument he can use to dissuade the paying customers from demanding more shooting. But to keep the peace he will have to use diplomacy and tact, both invaluable assets for any keeper.

At the end of the day the keeper and his assistants count the bag, separate young from old birds and distribute the customary brace, or more, to each Gun. The remainder are hung in the game larder waiting collection by the game dealer. The keeper will previously have given instructions for the collection of birds after each drive and their careful conveyance in the game cart. Grouse should not be simply popped into a sack and bundled into the back of a Land-Rover, to be sat on by dogs and kicked around by men's feet. Nor should pheasants and partridges for that matter, but in warm summer weather grouse need especially careful treatment, to prevent them spoiling and going 'high' before their time. It is usually a good idea to have the birds laid out on the ground at lunchtime, to help them to cool as well as to check the numbers.

The keeper will be responsible for paying off the staff, beaters, flankers and pickers-up, and will probably have to see that some of them are taken home.

Opposite **Game larder** The keeper in his game larder which is flyproof but airy and cool. It needs to be more carefully thought out than any old shed for a pheasant larder in winter

Opposite below **Loader and trailer for guns** A properly dressed loader removing a gun from the trailer, which also carries cartridges and shooting sticks. This design leaves more room for people and dogs in the vehicle

Below **Counting the bag** The bag is laid out to cool and to be counted by the keeper

Bottom **Pannier pony** The boy comes along the line of butts after the drive to collect the birds, which are usually left on top of the butt. Baskets on the pony allow air to circulate around the birds

Transport can itself be quite a headache for this Superman-of-all-trades. He will almost certainly have to arrange for the collection of several of the beaters early in the morning, unlike the pheasant shoots down south where most of the beaters turn up in their own cars.

The Guns require transport, too, and so does the lunch, and the drivers must be told where to go and at what time. The estate needs quite a big fleet of cars of one sort or other: Land-Rover, Range Rover for the Guns; for the beaters perhaps the Mercedes-engined Unimog of splendid performance; for decrepit oldies, who cannot walk up to their butts, a tracked vehicle like the Snowtrac, which also needs a trailer to save its tracks while travelling along roads. An alternative to tracks is a multiplicity of wheels, and the go-anywhere Argocat is a fine small-scale personnel carrier.

Foreign car manufacturers have come into the four-wheel-drive market recently with Mercedes G Series, Daihatsu and Subaru. Although the keeper will not have to bother about the boss's Chieftain Jeep or Datsun Patrol, all the others come under his authority and, incidentally, have to be looked after, cleaned and serviced between shoots and in the off season.

There may be trailers, too, acting as game carts or specially made to carry guns and cartridges. And trailers have a special propensity for developing flat tyres, with no spare, at the most awkward times, if they are not looked after.

In the old days transport was Shanks's pony, or a real four-footed load carrier, say a Fell pony or a Garron. These could take some of the elderly gentlemen up the hill, while the rest walked. Ponies were also, of course, used to carry stags down the hill after a successful stalk. A small left-over from these times, still happily met occasionally, is the pannier pony, whose leader collects up the birds after each drive. He walks along the gun line, where the birds have been left on top of the butts, and puts them in the baskets on each side of his pony; but he is one more problem for the keeper because of his slow speed over the ground (even if he does transfer his load to a motorized game cart when he reaches the road). If the Guns in their Land-Rovers are going to leave the Lodge at 9.00 a.m. and be in their butts at 9.30 a.m., what time must the pony boy set out?

And when they all come tearing off the hill at 5.00 p.m. to go to tea, or a bath, or a whisky and soda or the game larder, what time is the pony going to get back? This vexing problem may explain why shoots transfer their allegiance to the Haflinger, a strong Scandinavian pony – except that the modern version is a Volkswagen-engined, four-wheel-drive pick-up truck, an excellent game cart; practical, but not so picturesque as a sleek, sure-footed pony picking its way down the hill, both panniers full and a happy smile on the face of the lad leading it. What cares he if everybody else reached base two hours ago? Perhaps quite a lot, what with Coronation Street or the Test Match due on television, so maybe that is one more reason why we don't see the pannier pony more often.

Transport arrangements vary on different shoots but the Guns can usually be sure of reasonable comfort, and vehicles able to get them to the butts on time. A mild uncertainty arises over the numbers of wives, sons and loaders they may bring along, all hoping for a lift. Beaters deserve a roof over their heads, and at least straw bales to sit on; they do not always get them. If you hop a lift with the keeper, especially if he is in a hurry, you may have a rough ride: rattle, bang, crash in the back of a short-wheel-base Land-Rover or Daihatsu, a hard metal seat, no cushions and the floor awash with chains, empty cartridge boxes, Fenn traps, lunch haversacks, spare sticks and flags and a large jack; a couple of vast retrievers clamber over everything, swaying and falling, and scrambling up again to see where we are going; it is a canvas-roofed body with an open back, exhaust fumes waft in, and mud and rain splatter around; the small trailer on the back clanks and thumps, lurching wildly and threatening to turn over. Hang on to something, a roof strut will do, brace your legs against the opposite side; it is just as good exercise as walking, and very good for the tummy muscles!

Another important part of the organization is the provision of transport for the beaters between drives. It is not always possible to arrange owing to the terrain, but when it is it considerably cuts down the waiting time for the Guns. They may enjoy communing with Nature or having a snooze as they loll in their butts, but that tedious period during the long walk out by the beaters before they start back reduces the number of drives that can be done in the day; or means that everybody gets home later than they need in the evening. It is interesting that 100 years ago grouse shooters often stayed out till 8.00 p.m., caring less for their dinner than the theory that the birds were more easily found in the evening, when they congregated in their roosting areas. Nowadays there is usually more of an urgency to get back for drinks and baths.

Two other lesser worries for the keeper concern the blue hare and deer. The blue, or mountain hare, is smaller and slower than the brown hare of the lowlands; on a grouse-driving day it lollops slowly up to the butts and is by no means a sporting shot. Indeed, for safety reasons a rule of 'No ground game' is often in force. These hares are also considered to be less good eating than their brown counterparts; but shooting staff (beaters, loaders and pickers-up) who have come up from the south and are living in the bothy or camping in the grounds of the big house are a mite disappointed if there are no hares at the end of the day. A bit of free protein in the stew is always welcome!

Too many hares on a moor means a loss of food for grouse and sheep; indeed some estimates reckon that four or five hares consume as much grazing as one sheep. On the other hand a reasonable number of hares are acceptable because the foxes can eat *them* instead of turning their attentions to the grouse. The keeper will probably have to organize hare drives in the autumn to control numbers, although the market value of the carcasses is not likely to be high. A small gain for the estate may be the letting of hare shooting, by the day, in winter when the animals have turned white. This colour change, incidentally, is due to a moult of the animal's coat and not, as is sometimes said, to a direct alteration of pigment in the hairs. The hare undergoes three moults, brown to brown with grey-blue underfur, approximately June to September; brown to white, October to February, with the main moult usually finished by December; white to brown, February to May.

Deer are unlikely to be much trouble to the keeper since they usually keep to the highest ground. A deer 'forest', where the animals are encouraged for the stalking, is different territory from a grouse moor. Deer wander, of course, cross boundaries at will and on a moor they take some of the grazing. In winter they come down lower and in hard times may be some help to the grouse by trampling in the snow and breaking ice to allow the birds to reach the heather.

The keeper's job, then, is one of considerable responsibility. He may be helped a great deal by an owner living nearby, a sympathetic man able to supply advice *and* physical action. Conversely, the owner may live hundreds of miles away, the keeper having to deal with an agent who perhaps has little interest in or knowledge of the finer points of grouse management. In any event he is liable to have to live in fairly remote circumstances, although often in beautiful surroundings. It would be exceptionally bad luck if he were to be condemned to such a place as the mythical Auchenflichity. A tenant once took the shooting there and when he went up to see it, knowing little of it, he asked at the inn where he stayed, 'Do you know Auchenflichity?'

To which came the uncompromising reply, 'Aye.'

'And what sort of place is it?'

'Gin the De'il was tethered on it ye'd just say "Puir brute!"'

5 The Atmosphere

Have you ever seen a more beautiful dog than an English setter in action? Of course all breed owners have their favourites – greyhounds galloping across October stubble, a dark yellow labrador advancing down the side of a wood in November sunshine with a cock pheasant in its mouth, perhaps only a stumpy little terrier looking pleased about a killed rat. But consider the flowing, undulating movement of the setter, streaming through the heather, white and grey, or black and tan, an eye-catching contrast against the purple and the green. A couple of Guns following, each side of the dog's handler, and behind, a keeper with a retriever and possibly another setter on a leash.

The questing dog gallops over the ground, at times seems to fly, so smoothly and swiftly does it quarter its area. Until suddenly it stops. It might have been shot, except that it is too tensely alive, crouching, and staring intently towards the invisible birds in front. What's that thumping noise? It's your heart!

The handler moves forward and the dog 'draws on' to his point. Up springs the covey, one or other of the Guns fires, according to which side the birds fly, and the keeper gives the labrador a 'Hi-lost' to pick up. Sometimes, before the birds get up, the Guns may see heads bobbing up and down as the covey creeps through fairly short heather; the dog sees nothing, he is held in thrall by the secret power of his wonderful nose. At other times birds may erupt from totally unexpected places, perhaps even at your very feet. And one old bird, instead of taking off into the wind, waits until the last possible second and then suddenly shoots off behind, downwind. You have to be alert *all* the time.

Then the second setter is sent out while the first is rested, and we can admire again the amazing vital energy of these dogs, and the instinct bred into them, brought to perfection by superlative training. This is the original sport of grouse shooting, hunting man aided by the scarcely credible powers of the carefully developed dog. Incidentally, as a point of safety, never take a shot, should birds suddenly appear, unless you can *see* the dog; it might be hidden in a small hollow in the ground and suddenly emerge in the line of fire. Similarly, keep a good look all round for people, such as a handler with reserve dogs, because when put up the birds by no means always fly straight away to the front.

There are various ways to deploy the dogs. Often two work together; when one makes a point and the other comes galloping towards it, to freeze in its turn, it is said to 'back' the first dog. Reserve dogs are usually kept some distance behind the Guns, 100 yards or more, in the hope of calming down their zeal so that they are not worn out with nervous tension while waiting their turn. Although more Guns may accompany the dogs, two is really enough for the best sport, the only extras needed being a lad or two to carry the shot birds.

Spaniels hunting game are taught to drop to shot. Setters drop to wing, or flush, which means that as soon as the bird they are pointing gets up they lie down.

'Dogging', the word for pursuing grouse with the help of a pointer or setter, was originally carried out by the owner or tenant of a moor, and his friends who knew the area and the finer points of procedure. The modern Gun who has rented a few days' shooting should remember three golden rules: keep quiet; keep up with the dogs; and have faith in the keeper and handler in working the right areas to find the birds. Much of the skill in dogging lies in knowing where the birds are likely to be in various weather conditions. It is usual to start on the higher ground and work down, expecting the more profitable shooting to be in the evening when the birds are in the best feeding areas. Later in the season, as the birds become wilder, it may be necessary to work the dogs downwind instead of the more

Dogging The dogging party moves out at the start of the day. The girl handler has just sent out her setter; two Guns follow with a keeper and boy to mind the retrievers and the next dogs to be sent out

Above **English setter on point** The dog remains rigid until encouraged by handler to move forward

Right **Drawing on** The handler encourages the setter to move forwards towards the birds

normal diagonally across and upwind; Guns should understand the need for this and the consequent extra difficulty for the dogs. They should also appreciate that the easiest walking, often along the contours and regardless of the wind, is not the best for the dogs, whose needs should have priority.

As to the differences between setters and pointers, their own protagonists will argue from now until next season. Many unprejudiced admirers consider that setters are hardier and can range further and for a longer time over the tough terrain of a Highland moor; but they will also say that pointers last better on a hot August day and are easier to train. A setter 'sets' by crouching when it has winded game, and a pointer 'points', standing upright and with one forepaw raised. Of course, many dogs will point, and labradors and spaniels quite frequently do so – for instance, when marking a wounded bird in a bush.

There once was a little pointer bitch that was particularly anxious always to please her owner. When there were folds in the ground, so that the dogs sometimes came on point out of sight of Guns and handler, this bitch did not remain in the classic rigid position, but after a few moments used to run back to her handler, wag her tail signifying, 'I've found something over there,' and then creep back to the point. Not Field Trial behaviour, but useful and somewhat endearing. Pointers can be very sensitive dogs and if they think they have displeased their handler will sometimes go wrong and hunt quite haphazardly instead of quartering correctly.

Field Trials for these dogs often take place in July, before the shooting season, when birds are put up and a gun is fired. These events can be a help to the owner of the ground in determining what stock it holds.

'Bird dogs', as the type is called in the USA, do not have to be only English setters and pointers. There is also the Irish setter, of beautiful mahogany colour, although originally it was white and red; the black and tan Gordon setter; the German short-haired pointer; the Hungarian Vizsla and the Weimaranar. These last three are collectively known as HPRs because they Hunt, Point and Retrieve. They do this most successfully on partridge and pheasant shoots in the south, but are less often seen on grouse moors. It is still possible to hire dogs, with or without handlers, if you rent a moor for a week or two or for the season. Owners of HPRs, of course, can bring and work their own dogs.

The curious feature, to the outsider, of dogging for grouse is that the dogs do not retrieve the shot birds. They used to, and in the nineteenth century many owners considered the dogs deserved the reward of picking up the grouse after all the hard work they put in to find them. But it became fashionable to bring out retrievers to attend to that task, simply to allow the setters to go to work again immediately and find more grouse. And this has become traditional. On the Continent pointers are expected to follow the trail of wounded deer or boar and retrieve duck, pheasant, partridge or fox, having originally hunted over the ground and pointed the game! Much the same occurs in the States, and in close country the dogs sometimes carry small bells which the handler hears as they work through the cover: when the bell stops tinkling the dog is on point.

All of which is some way from that old traditional method of seeking grouse on a British moor. Perhaps the die-hards may comment, 'We've got a unique bird, so why shouldn't we "hunt" it, as you'd say, in our own way?' Some trainers might also admit that they are quite happy *not* to let their dogs do any retrieving because it reduces the temptation for them to run in.

If you shoot grouse over dogs you will be fascinated by their scenting powers. How *do* they do it? What are good scenting conditions? Rain beforehand to tamp down the pollen on the heather? Or dry warm days? Foxhunters argue merrily on these problems, and breed their hounds for the best scenting ability, allied to stamina; and so indeed do grouse 'hunters'.

Retrieving dogs, and those which hunt, like spaniels, search for body scent, sometimes amplified by blood scent when the bird has been shot. Mostly they seek their game with heads low, taking the scent off the ground. Bird dogs, however, take air scent with their heads held high; even when the game moves forward and the dog 'roads up' (advances) his nose is high enough to catch the air scent, not low like a bloodhound following a ground trail. It is similar to foxhounds on a very fast hunt with a 'breast high' scent, although the bird dog not only follows this scent, he also picks it up in the first place at full gallop. After the flush the dog may be allowed to move up to the 'haunt', where the birds were, and enjoy a rewarding sniff or two.

As a matter of interest, many of the old words have gone out of fashion now; few trainers, for example, still use the word 'Toho' as a command for the dog to stop. The action of the dog moving forward after it is on point is variously described as 'drawing on', 'roading up' or 'roading in'. A trainer watching an animal working might say, 'That dog roads in nice.' When you ask how he trains the dog to do that he replies, 'Ye jist tell 'im ter go on, like.'

Sometimes the dog makes a mistake, and the game turns out to be a lark. Or the game might not squat in front of the dog, but scuttle away through the heather; from point to flush may be a hundred yards or more. This is incredibly thrilling for the Guns and calls for steady nerves to make a successful shot when the time comes.

Another feature about scent is that the sitting hen, in common with most birds while brooding, exudes almost no smell and dogs can easily pass very close without winding her. Birds resting around the middle of the day, having fed in the morning, with their feathers tucked close into their bodies, also have less scent than when they are moving through the heather. Consequently it can be more profitable to search for the birds in the evening, while they are feeding, than at noon when they are resting. Conversely, for the same reasons it may be considered unsporting to shoot them in the evening; it depends on the stock available and how many the owner wants killed.

Scent is always inexplicable to humans; one day your retriever may be galloping along beside a hedge when it suddenly stops, its head jerked round almost severely enough to break its neck. It dives into the hedge, battles through nettles and brambles and emerges with a partridge. On another occasion a large dead cock pheasant is lying out on open plough, and when sent for it the dog seems unable to locate it, even when so close as to be practically standing on it.

Dogging for grouse is best done in fair weather, a warm day with a light breeze. Rain spoils the sport, partly because the birds leave the saturated cover of the thicker heather and stay out in the open, where they see the dogs and tend to depart before the shooting party can get within range.

This, the first method of getting a shot at grouse, has a charm which its devotees find unbeatable, but they would also admit that the actual shooting does not require the same skill as in driving. It can be strenuous, but it is not such hard work as walking-up.

Walking in line involves half a dozen or more Guns interspersed with keepers, boys, wives and any other persuadable accomplices. You do see the country, but you also have to cover a big acreage! As you have no dogs to find the birds and you do not know where they are, you have to look everywhere: pushing through the knee-high heather, while your neighbour on an old burnt patch has an easy stroll; jumping down into a gully and scrabbling up the other side; slipping sideways on the steep slopes covered in bilberry bushes. Rocks, peat hags, tall bracken and tussocky grass combine to make the walking both interesting and exhausting. The shots may be fairly easy but the shooting, from an uncertain stance and probably when out of breath, is often fraught with problems. Somebody has to carry spare cartridges and the shot birds, as well as working the retrievers to find them. Some of the party will often be out of sight of the others when a shot is taken and then the line must stop; after the pick-up a whistle is blown to signal the restart. At all times the line itself should keep straight otherwise stragglers may become news items: 'Sportsman shot on grouse moor'.

Walking without pointing dogs is the least expensive way of shooting grouse; and, as you walk, the moor spins its magic around you. The wind on your face, bending the long dry grass; bilberry leaves turning to red and gold, and then the blackened burnt places with sun-bleached grey twigs that crackle as you walk over them. The bright, clean green of the young heather, the best sustenance for the grouse and also for the bleating sheep that scurry away as your party approaches. Then into the older heather, thick and tall, quite heavy walking even on the flat. Little boggy patches, soft peat and moss; and ahead that staggering view of miles and miles of sweeping country with dramatic storm clouds giving way to shafts of sun on the distant hills,

alking up Guns, friends and dogs make up the line with someone in charge to try keep it straight

zsla retrieving grouse Many pickers-up are glad to come to the moors in paration for their dogs entering for Field Trials

slatey and purple in the rainlight. And the anticipation, hope, indeed fear that at any moment grouse will erupt in front of you, or even behind. Walking-up and shooting over dogs are great ways of teaching young and inexperienced Guns what may be termed moorcraft.

Incidentally, in the nineteenth century if birds were too wild to be approachable it was common practice to fly a kite over the moor. This resembled a hawk and made the grouse sit tight, but nobody seems to try it these days.

Many moors start the season walking, with or without dogs, and only begin driving at the end of August. The choice may be traditional, or due to a wish to do a sort of armed reconnaissance to estimate the stock more accurately. Or because if you are going to walk and drive it is better to walk first and then, when the birds become too wild to be approachable, start driving. Some dogging enthusiasts like to drive first because they consider that shooting over pointers and setters is much more worthwhile after the 'threat' of hot weather in August has passed.

When the birds start packing, usually about September, dogging and walking-up become impossible. In the north of Scotland grouse are generally more backward than in the warmer south and are less inclined to pack. This is one of the main reasons for the popularity of dogging in those parts; others are the difficulty of obtaining sufficient beaters, and transporting them, and the fact that there are usually insufficient birds to make driving economic. Probably a traditional tendency to support dogging in the north came from the fact that the area had many deer forests where hawks were accepted – that is, not shot. This meant that grouse tended by habit to squat and hide rather than fly, and so were more approachable by dogs.

An important point anywhere is the comparative effects on the stock of walking and driving. Experts who shoot over dogs will tell you, 'When the covey gets up, take the cock bird first; then the hen, and afterwards one or two of the youngsters.' And they are skilful enough to practise what they preach.

Duffers, and average shots, and even experienced good shots when walking without dogs, confronted by a swiftly scattering covey, are almost sure to shoot at the nearest birds: the young ones. Older birds, barren pairs or single cocks, tend to rise when out of range.

On the other hand, when driven the parents lead the covey and so are generally the first to be shot. Driving also tends to mix up the coveys which is beneficial for future breeding stock. In a good breeding year, when the moor should be shot hard, it is best done by driving; when walking-up, big bags cannot be made after the birds become wild and fly before the Guns can get close enough. Sometimes drives are taken back and forth over the same butts, perhaps all day. This thoroughly mixes up the families of birds and also increases the likelihood of killing the old birds, which keep flying, while the exhausted young ones sit tight and remain hidden from the beaters.

Driven grouse: as you wait for them you cannot help absorbing some of the feel of the moor. It is a hot August day and the fine views of the distant hills are washed pale in the haze. The heather is brilliant purple, smelling of honey, and the pollen gets on the dogs' fur and on everyone's boots. There is a hum of insect life and dancing black flies bob up and down. Red admiral and peacock butterflies flit past and the little harebell growing beside the butt bends in the gentle breeze. Bees are busy, daddy-longlegs flutter around and ewes and their lambs go 'baare-baare' in several different keys. Grey boulders pock-marked with green and black lichen litter the landscape, itself a patchwork of flowering heather and black skeleton-like stems, green grass and bracken, with the brown gravel road twisting away into the distance; far below on one side stretches the gold of ripening cornfields.

You think back to the rendezvous at the beginning of the day by the keeper's cottage. The under-keepers are there with their dogs, and the low-ground keepers, having seen to their pheasants first. They wear heavy black studded boots with the toes turned up in a curious way; their suits are smart, all the same pattern, the laird's plaid if we are north of the border or, more prosaically, the owner's choice of a tweed he likes if it is further south. The beaters stand around chattering as they wait, stowing their lunch satchels and Thermos flasks in the transport, collecting their flags rolled round sticks. The loaders form another group; some already have guns and cartridges, others

Driven grouse The grouse come over the butt at different heights and angles

Left **The Picker-up** A good delivery to the picker-up. His other two dogs watch; one of them also has a bird

still await the arrival of their bosses; they are a little less exuberant than the beaters, more serious, as befits their job perhaps. Whereas the beaters wear all manner of garb, jerseys, jeans, T-shirts, anoraks, the loaders are a smarter company – some very smart, with proper shooting suits and handsome tough brogues with a big fringed tongue hanging over the laces.

The pickers-up form another group: a shooting farmer, grabbing a day off from harvesting, with his wise old labrador; a retired soldier, with two springer spaniels; a young matron explaining in a county voice how she simply *had* to come, with her sleek black two-year-old labrador, even if it did mean leaving the month-old baby at home; and a professional handler, well known at Field Trials, with four retrievers.

With all the Guns assembled and the beaters gone ahead, the party moves off, one Land-Rover towing a trailer specially fitted with compartments for carrying guns; it has skids as well as wheels, you notice, for use over snow in the winter, when its load is tools for the keeper's many jobs. Drawing away from the house you catch the flash of bright rowan berries on a little tree by the track, a happy sight as memorable as that evocative smell of burnt honey when the Land-Rovers stop, and their hot exhausts smoke from close contact with heather and peat.

And here we are in the butts. The long wait ends when your neighbour whistles a warning, and suddenly the grouse are coming straight at you, swiftly silent and somehow rather darkly sinister. You shoot.

How you shoot is dealt with in the next chapter; it is certainly different from other forms of shooting. Meantime, among other things to be considered, how about the weather?

By no means is it always hot and sunny; nor does a day that starts that way remain so. Hailstones as big as good garden peas can mark the end of a glorious day in Perthshire; or in Morayshire it can rain so solidly all day long that the sunken butts on the low ground get full of water and you think you will soon be suffering from trench foot. High up the hill in Berwickshire the Scotch mist is so thick that the day's shooting has to be cancelled, while down in Durham there is a cold, cold deluge that soaks into the bones and the owner calls it a day at lunchtime, if only out of sympathy for the wretched, teeth-chattering beaters. In Yorkshire the heavy black clouds are so low it is almost dark, and a howling gale tears across Cumbria, threatening to blow all the birds across to the North Sea. This is not just a fair-weather sport, an affair of indolent ease with transport right up to the butts and polished brogues that never get dirty. Frequently long stiff climbs are necessary in order to reach the butts, and very often the weather operates in extremes: heat and flies or high winds and downpours. But for variety of scenery, for memorable sights and sounds and smells, and for blood-tingling excitement and nerve-tweaking uncertainty there is no shooting to compare with driven grouse, the truly wild bird.

Battered by the wind swishing like waves on the shore, or roasting in the gorgeous summer sunshine, many people are involved; and one important item for all of them is lunch.

This can be very much al fresco, everyone sitting on the ground and munching sandwiches helped along with a flask of tea or a bottle of beer. For the beaters and flankers and pickers-up it very often is little more than that. Some shoots offer the Guns similar treatment, except that hampers are brought up with a bigger selection of edibles. Trestle tables appear from which you can help yourself, standing up; and if it is belting with rain you still stand up, or, if you are lucky, hop into a Land-Rover. But the best and jolliest lunches are in a bothy, or lunch-hut, which may be a tin shed or a sturdy stone building, with a long table and bench seats. Here, amid a welter of coats hanging on pegs and dogs under foot, all manner of goodies appear. Mutton soup in Tupperware beakers, cottage pies, steak and kidney pie with potatoes and carrots; cold salmon, turkey, chicken, ham, sausages; salads with peppers and grapes; rich rummy fruit cake, Stilton cheese and rolls and biscuits, Bakewell tarts and mince pies. Before the meal and with it there is pretty well any drink you want and port, sloe gin and coffee to follow. In the close quarters of this jovial atmosphere the cheerful talk covers a multitude of subjects – even when, as sometimes happens, the host bans alcohol, or at any rate hard liquor, on the hill in the interests of safety.

Tall stories or, more likely, good-natured leg pulling, share

Rough country This is mildly rough country for the Guns and their loaders to negotiate on their way up to the butts. It can be a great deal more strenuous than just walking along a flat, grassy field

Wing Shapes Flying grouse showing their wings in all sorts of different attitudes

Lunch break Warm August weather as the elite of the party, the keepers and flankers, take their lunchtime sandwiches in the sun

The end of a drive As the
beaters approach the butts a
few sheep pass between
them. Sometimes two
teams of beaters are
employed and as the first
team finishes its drive the
second is already out in
position a couple of miles
away ready to begin a new
drive from the opposite
direction

Left **A well-dressed lady
Gun in the butt** Notice the
marker posts each side. Pity
the loader isn't wearing a
hat

Right **Loader**, watching the
birds in front, seems to be
pointing the gun at the
shooter's back

places with City news, cures for gout and possibly a little fashion talk and gossip among the ladies.

'I was given a loader once,' remarks one of the Guns. 'Turned out he'd never been one before, he was a gardener or something. I managed to take two out of the first lot of birds that came over, and when I turned for my second gun this chap said, "I got one, how many did you?"'

Another tells of a talkative butt companion who was nonetheless an excellent loader and a keen wildfowler. 'He told me a yarn,' he says, 'went something like this: "I were down on the marshes one day wi' the tide comin' in, and in front o' me were a little mound. Soon this 'ere mound is surrounded b' water an' up pops a little ol' 'are outa the grass there. I waits for un to come ashore but as water rises 'er starts out seawards. There was biggish waves and I lets fly when I could see 'er but as I fires a wave come up and 'ides 'er. I lets fly several shots but 'tis no good. So I does opposite like, and fires when I can't see 'er. An' I shoots that ol' 'are stone dead!"'

Shotguns and shooting schools are other likely subjects: 'Those people at Bolland and Folland don't know a thing! When I went to their practice grouse butt they never told me the birds flew like these do!'

'Ah, yes – did I tell you that after Hurdie's overhauled my guns I had a broken striker the first time I used them?'

'My godson has a Moss, belonged to his grandfather, says it's a marvellous gun for grouse. You know why? Because it's had so much use the choke's all worn away; it's just a plain tube!'

'Clay shooting's no help to grouse shooting. The wretched clays keep slowing down.'

Meanwhile, authority will be keeping an eye on the clock, for few things are worse than keeping the beaters waiting needlessly. And soon the host announces, 'Right, we must move off in five minutes please.'

And so we return to the sights and sounds of the afternoon's drives. Those far-away slowly moving white dots, that you know must indicate beaters, gradually vanish as they walk down behind a crest, to appear again much closer, so that you can hear the crack of their flags; then the urgent whistle as one of the Guns gives a warning of approaching birds; and the sudden appearance of the flankers, who bob up in unexpected places, brandishing their flags, and then subside again. It is a setting that never fails to entrance, providing the backdrop for the arrival of the chief actors, the birds.

It is interesting to see how the unique atmosphere evoked by the sight of them in flight is transferred on to canvas by the painter.

The eye of an artist is indeed a marvellous gift, but why do painters rarely portray correctly how grouse look in flight? A round shape with an arc over it is the generally accepted form of a flying grouse as it approaches the shooter in his butt. But does it never look otherwise? Wings flapping up for a change? They cannot always be on the downward sweep.

Figure 5

Archibald Thorburn's picture, *The Butts in Sight* (1913), shows only three out of twenty-three birds with wings *not* in what we might call the basic position.

J. C. Harrison, a modern artist well known to wildfowlers, painted an exciting picture called *Grouse at Full Speed*. It shows six birds zooming straight at you, and every one is in the basic position. It is marvellously evocative of a moor and those wild free spirits which can appear so suddenly.

Brian Rawling had an exhibition of his paintings in London in November 1974. In one, *Grouse over Glenavon*, out of eleven birds only two are not depicted with their wings in the basic attitude. Charles Whymper, who lived at the end of the last century, painted a fine picture called *Grouse on the Wing* with fifty-three birds all in the same wing position.

As anyone who observes grouse or has seen photographs of them will know, it is exceptional for more than a few birds in a covey to have their wings in that basic position; most grouse just do *not* fly like that all the time.

Of course modern wildlife artists are not unaware of this; nearly all of them are knowledgeable naturalists and they know what grouse really look like but they also know what the public expects the birds to look like. The basic position is the gliding attitude, the most easily seen, with no rapid wing beats, often because the bird is already going so fast that any more flapping would not increase its speed. That is how you recognize a grouse, it is typical; birds portrayed with their wings in other attitudes might be mistaken by the untutored public for a bunch of rooks or starlings. And so we have a little artistic licence in most paintings, to awaken a mental picture, and provide something far more pleasing to hang on the wall than strictly accurate shapes, which cannot convey the same atmosphere.

Highland Raiders, by J. Farquharson (1900) shows grouse feeding on corn stooks in the foreground; beyond are eighteen more birds approaching, all of them in the basic position. They look aesthetically pleasing, with more visual appeal than the truthful, haphazard pattern of wing shapes that would be revealed by a camera. For accuracy's sake photographs show what flying grouse look like, but the artist's eye creates a more beautiful picture, and catches the atmosphere that the beholder expects. And perhaps it should be admitted that the painter is usually portraying a tranquil scene whereas birds photographed on a shoot are often taking evasive action!

6 The Shooting

A standard game gun is most suitable for grouse shooting, and this means a double-barrelled side-by-side 12 bore with 28-inch barrels. It will be bored improved cylinder and about half choke, and weigh around 6½ pounds. Variations are perfectly permissible but a gun with considerable choke, normally used for wildfowling or high pheasants, puts its user at a disadvantage when he is trying to intercept driven grouse dodging past his butt at short range.

Self-opening guns are an advantage when the pace is hot and loading must be done as quickly as possible. In such a gun the barrels drop, through the assertion of its main spring or an auxiliary spring, when the top lever is moved across; there is no need for the barrels to be pushed down by the operator. This feature is usually found only in best guns.

Repeaters and automatics can be used to shoot grouse, although it is a convention that they will never be loaded with more than two cartridges. They are not popular on shoots in the United Kingdom, largely because the barrels cannot be dropped to indicate that they are unloaded.

The action of opening a normal shotgun cocks it and also applies the safety-catch. On some guns, however, the safety-catch is not automatically operated and has to be put on by the user. This is potentially dangerous, particularly if such a gun is used with a loader who may not be aware of this somewhat non-standard feature.

As with all shotgun shooting, the gun must fit the user and a point to consider here is that the original fitting may have been

Grouse suddenly appear over a wall

Close birds The range is so short that the Gun cannot really be going to shoot the birds as close as this; he can swing round and take them behind a little further away. But there is certainly no need for heavily choked barrels

done in the winter when the user was wearing thicker clothing than he might expect to need in August.

A sleeve for the gun protects it in the transport, and a sling is an enormous help in carrying it up the sometimes quite considerable distances to the butts. Cartridge bags are essential and the cartridges themselves should be standard loads and probably number 7 shot. Certainly no 'high velocity' or 'magnum loads' are required.

Some shoots issue a card to each Gun which tells him the number of his butt for each drive. The numbers may be chosen by the host according to the importance and seniority of his guests, or perhaps their infirmity when faced with a stiff climb, or any other whim he fancies! It is more usual, however, in an attempt to give each shooter equal opportunity to be in the centre butts, where more birds may be expected, to draw for numbers at the beginning of the day, and then to change numbers after each drive. The most common way of changing is to add two to one's number; thus if you start at number 2 on the first drive you become number 4, 6, 8 and 2 again on subsequent drives. A more cunning way of doing it, so that individuals have different neighbours throughout the day, is for odd numbers to move up two places and even numbers down until they reach the end of the line, when they start moving back in the opposite direction. It sounds a bit like the intricate steps in an esoteric country dance, but it can be achieved without too much brain strain, even after lunch, like this: number 4 subsequently becomes number 6, 8, 7, 5, 3, 1, 2, 4; number 5 moves to number 3, 1, 2, 4, 6, 8, 7, 5. With an odd number of Guns the principle can still be followed, the last move towards the end of the line being one place instead of two. Supposing there are nine Guns, the even-numbered gentleman moves from number 8 to 9, there being no number 10, and then works his way back on the odd numbers. Most shoots number from the right but some preserve a mysterious tradition of their own and number from the left; some even keep number 1 always at the top of the hill. Bemused guests are best advised to stand helplessly until manoeuvred in the right direction by host, syndicate leader, shoot manager or the driver of the Land-Rover.

Driven grouse provide a form of shooting especially their

own, and it needs studying. Here are a few points for the first-timer in a grouse butt:

1 Make sure that the front of your butt is truly in line with the others.
2 Have a look round to see if any flankers are within range, and also any pickers-up (who may be directly behind you).
3 Study the ground in front and think about the wind which will affect the way the birds are likely to approach and cross the butts.
4 Decide where in front the grouse will be in range. If you are a beginner, and everybody knows it, there is no need to be shy of checking distance. If your host is agreeable (some are not), walk out 40 yards and note some feature to use as a mark: a rock, mossy patch, change in colour of the grass and heather, or whatever it may be.
5 Check the tidy organization of the rest of your small world in the butt; everything has its correct, convenient and least obstructive place. Wife, loader, dog, cartridges, shooting stick, coat, marker for fall of birds.
6 Keep quiet; no shouted banter to neighbouring butts. Nearby grouse will hear and depart out of the drive.
7 Take note of any marker sticks on top of the butt, indicating dangerous shooting areas, and also of any post which could show where a neighbouring butt is out of sight owing to a dip in the ground.

When you have settled in the butt, watch your front but do not tire your eyes searching for birds long before they are likely to appear. At the same time you should remember that grouse tend to keep low and are often difficult to see against a background of heather. When the birds do come do not hide behind the parapet of the butt and then pop up like a jack-in-the-box; stand up and keep still, so that the covey comes on and does not scatter while still out of range. The birds are used to seeing the butts and drab figures showing over the top will not alarm them. But sudden movement will.

Try to take your first bird as far out as you reasonably can; if you pick it up over the ends of your barrels at about 60 yards it will be only 40 yards out by the time you shoot, close enough

Grouse approaching Raise the gun and decide which one to take. Note the road winding over the moor to the left

Birds close to the butt They are almost on the butt and they all seem to be going in different directions. Which one have you chosen? Hang on to it!

Above **Aerobatics** The man raises his gun and the grouse puts on a smart flying display to outwit him

Left **Low grouse** Sometimes grouse fly very low. This one nipped past the butt so low that the Gun failed to see it in time and has not yet got his gun up

Right **High grouse** Grouse can fly high and offer unusual targets when driven from one ridge to another, with the Guns standing in the valley between

Good loading drill All looking the right way: Gun towards the birds, loader at what he is doing (*not* at the birds), dogs looking back at what has just been shot

Pair guns using a loader. One dead bird top left; the others fly all ways. Grouse do not fly straight like pheasants. Note the Gun's leather 'western' type hat

for an approaching bird. It is also better to concentrate on having one good shot in front and not try to fire off both barrels in a hurry. Much depends on whether you experience a rather poor drive, with a dozen or so birds coming your way, or whether you have been dropped in the deep end and hundreds come over. If the latter it will very likely seem impossible to get the gun off at all as the birds hurtle by from all angles; and then all too easy to bang away at no more than the turbulence the birds leave behind them.

When you have time to think, and when you have been grouse shooting more often, you will develop a reasonably simple drill which surprisingly often produces good results. Here are some more principles to try to follow·

1 Choose the bird you are going to shoot, and hang on to it. Do not be diverted.
2 Line up the gun muzzles on that bird and shoot as soon as the butt meets your shoulder.
3 Do not turn round for a shot behind while grouse are still coming from in front. It is not worth shooting away at long-range, fast disappearing, oblique downward skimming birds when, if you just turn back to your front, you will find some comparatively easy direct approachers.
4 When you do shoot behind, do it quickly. Departing birds shot at long range are only pricked. The time to take the long shot is while the birds are coming towards you. It is a good principle always to try to shoot off both barrels in front if there is more than one bird; once the habit is acquired of turning round for the second barrel, trouble is in store when many birds come over in a pack.
5 If birds drop down in front of the butts, have a bang at them as they settle; no good waiting for a sitter – they will be lost in the heather! If the birds are left they will soon attract their friends and relations, and when they do get up the whole lot will go out to a flank or nip back over the beaters' heads.

Grouse can fly most mysteriously. They can appear from nowhere and practically take your hat off; or be in sight for half a mile as they seem to be aiming straight at your eyes; then, suddenly, they veer and have gone. And they do not squawk as they rise or quack or honk a warning as they fly towards you! Although, in fact, late in the season birds do sometimes call as they approach.

Driven grouse offer every imaginable type of shot. It is the most difficult form of shotgun shooting. The birds fly unpredictably and rarely straight; after several wing beats they usually glide and swerve and then flap again, and when alarmed their aerobatics are phenomenal. Very often they fly low, much lower than most game shooters expect at first; plenty of experience of pheasants, partridges, duck or pigeon can still leave the sportsman aghast at the head-high hustling of his first grouse. Even after he has had a fair amount of experience of August birds, their extra wildness in October will test his skill to the uttermost.

Another hazard, because of this low flying propensity, is the danger caused by the possibility of shooting down the line of butts. More about the whole safety aspect later, but it can cause the shooter to hesitate, and when a man has any doubt about a shot it is a dead cert that he will miss.

Speed in shooting is essential to being a good grouse shot. Never must the Gun dwell in the aim, trying to make sure; this is poking, and it ensures a miss. A good piece of advice, culled from men of much experience, is, 'Lean forward as you shoot and think of trying to catch the bird in your left hand.' And you should also always rotate your body from the hips and not swing the arms across the body.

Well now, what's next? The real beginner at driven grouse is best placed in a flank butt with one gun and allowed to find his own feet, with the single admonition to shoot in *front*, and not turn round.

For a successful shoot, with the maximum bag, pair guns are needed, and here we come to the duties and skills of the loader. He has carried the guns up to the butt, taken them out of their sleeves, and opened up his bulky cartridge bag. The Gun should have armed himself with at least a handful of cartridges, in case of urgent need, and he may consider the small problem of whether to put them in the right pocket or left. If he is shooting only one gun and the loader is but a carrier this becomes more important. There is not a lot to it, but a difference exists between opening the gun with the right thumb, holding it at the grip and feeling in one's left jacket pocket for a cartridge, and opening the gun right handed, holding the dropped down barrels in the left hand and taking the cartridges from the right pocket and so loading them right handed. Consider for a moment, and then make your choice.

Shooting two guns with a loader requires practice and a recognized drill. In the confines of a grouse butt it also demands an understanding between the two participants as to where the loader positions himself; normally it should be to the right rear of the shooter who passes the fired gun past his right shoulder. Even when the shooter swings away round to his left for a shot, it is better that he should turn back to face his normal front before handing the gun to the loader. Dancing round in a circle can get them both in a terrible muddle.

Here is a good drill for loading:

1 Having fired one or both barrels the shooter puts on the safety catch and brings the gun back, muzzles up, and held in his right hand so that the breech is about level with his right shoulder.
2 The shooter holds his left hand out beyond the gun, palm open and facing his rear. Meanwhile he continues to watch his front, looking for approaching birds.
3 The loader takes hold of the empty, or partially empty, gun a few inches above the breech and at the same time places the loaded gun in the shooter's left hand.
4 The shooter grasps the fresh gun around the fore-end and prepares for his next shot.
5 The loader turns slightly to his right, lowers the gun so that the stock comes under his right arm, and he can flick it open with his thumb against the top lever and fingers pressing the side of the lock.
6 If the gun is not a self-opener the loader pushes down the barrels to eject the cartridges, while his right hand holds fresh cartridges.
7 Dropping the cartridges into the breech, the loader raises the stock with his right fingers a few inches behind the

trigger guard and then lifts the gun up vertically, holding it with his right hand at the grip.

8 The loader then turns his body slightly left and is ready to put the loaded gun into the shooter's left hand, and to take the fired gun at the same time.

Note that the guns are passed across with safety catches on. While waiting for birds to appear gun barrels should be pointing up in the air. There is not room in a butt for them to be pointing groundwards with any safety.

Most loaders have some sort of way of holding cartridges between their fingers to quicken up the action of loading the gun, replenishing from their bag immediately afterwards. If you are shooting alone it is possible to fire remarkably quickly if you hold spare cartridges like this: between the third and fourth fingers of the left hand, one cartridge with the crimp end pointing inwards, towards you; another cartridge between the same fingers of the right hand, crimp end pointing outwards. These cartridges do not interfere with gun handling, and having fired and opened the gun, by putting the left hand palm down over the breech you can pop its cartridge into the chamber, followed by the right hand's. With a little practice four rounds can be shot off with scarcely any delay, although not as fast as with an efficient loader. Then the classic performance is five out of a covey: a long left barrel as they approach; change guns and a left and right in front; change guns and a right and left behind. Things can become quite brisk at times.

One day a Gun took a bird in front and immediately turned for one behind. The first bird hit him smack on the head and he fell down, somewhat shocked. His loader helped him to his feet and, dazed and angry, the Gun asked, 'Didn't you see that bird coming?' to which the loader replied, 'Yes, sir, I saw it coming, and hid behind you!'

It is important to try to remember where shot birds fall, and sometimes markers are provided. These may take the form of a disc about 4 inches across, and marked into segments on which a cross can be pencilled in to mark the fall. If the action becomes too hot to record every bird, at least keep a running total in your head so that you know how many to look for after the drive. In

ar muffs Protection for the ears is recommended as long as it does not interfere with hearing such warnings as the whistle to stop shooting in front. The loader here taking awkward evasive action; perhaps the butt is a bit small

ame plotter This disc, placed on top of the butt and marked when opportunity lows, helps the Gun remember where the birds fell

A dangerous shot The gun is swinging ahead of the bird and it points at the next butt

Correct drill The shooter lifts his gun and follows the bird raising the gun-butt only when it is safe to shoot

hot down the line It should miss the nearest butt, although it could endanger
next one

the old days individual totals were considered of supreme importance, far more than they are now. The competitiveness was amazing, everyone seemed to dash about picking up birds, beginning even before the beaters reached the butt line! It was commonplace for all individual scores to be noted by the host, recorded in his Game Book and mentioned in letters to the editor when writing to the sporting press. Nowadays, although everyone wants to ensure that shot birds are picked up, it is all done in a more friendly way, with as much co-operation as possible. There is no room for selfishness in the shooting field. One reason a host might ask his Guns how many birds they had would be to form a good guess of the total bag, especially if he suspected that the beaters were stealing some.

Shooting driven grouse can be remarkably dangerous, if the participants are not specially careful. In the heat of the fray even the most experienced shots make mistakes. The chief error is swinging the gun across at a low bird so that it points down the line of butts; this happens more often than you may suppose. Marker sticks on the sides of the butts are a deterrent, but no guarantee for safe shooting; they should never be regarded as casting aspersions at a Gun's safe behaviour. They should, by rights, be placed by the Gun himself since their positioning depends on precisely where he stands.

Butts are rarely at the same level, and an uphill butt is always in danger of being peppered by a careless shooter lower down the hill; he may think he is swinging safely on to a fairly high bird only to find his gun muzzles pointing at his neighbour's head. Except that he will not discover it until he has fired, and by then an accident may have happened; distressingly often it is a pellet in the eye.

Shooting accidents are nearly always inexcusable. Often they are caused by greediness and sometimes by old age and slow reactions. Their likelihood may be increased by recklessness, possibly alcohol induced. They are never funny, although occasionally scarcely credible in the manner of their perpetration and in the small harm that befalls the victims.

One such incident concerned a foreign gentleman occupying number 8 butt. In number 9 was the laird's son, being coached by the factor. Most of the birds crossed the centre or right hand end of the line but a few came the gentleman's way; he had three shots. The first dropped a bird but also hit a flanker; the second hit a grouse, the laird's son and the factor, and the third also scored, including a beater. At the end of the drive the visitor proclaimed, 'I shoot them all, all the grouse and all the people!'

As the beaters approach it is customary for the Guns to cease shooting in front and only take the birds after they have crossed the butts line. Indeed, this is often mandatory, the order being announced by sounding a horn or whistle. It does not mean, however, that the Guns have to turn round, face the rear and wait for birds to fly over their shoulder, like a Skeet shot, Station 1, High House. Newcomers, nobly trying to do the right thing, have been known to adopt this curious procedure. Correct drill is to remain facing the front, collect any approaching bird over your left hand, gun muzzles up and butt well down by your hip; then turn around, watching the bird all the time, bringing up the butt to the shoulder as the bird flies into a safe zone.

On one occasion the beaters were quite close towards the end of a drive and a single grouse got up, going straight over a Gun's head. He was turning to take it behind when the Gun on his right shot it. His left hand neighbour, also of course in the line of fire, called out, 'Smart shot, William Tell!'

Safety, in fact, is the most important aspect of shotgun shooting. Better by far to be a safe shot than a brilliant one; everyone can achieve the former but very few the latter. At the end of a drive all guns are unloaded. No shooting at all, for any reason, can be countenanced between drives.

Competitiveness must never obtrude on a grouse shoot, especially among newcomers. The desire to shoot more than his neighbour can lead a man into taking appalling risks, even, for instance, to lifting his gun deliberately over the safety sticks on the butt, and waiting to shoot one of the last birds of the drive. The ability to pay to shoot is no substitute for the care and attention to details of behaviour shown by sportsmen with a lifetime's experience.

When walking-up or dogging the standard safety rules apply, particularly to the way the gun is carried. It *must* have its barrels pointing up in the air or down towards the ground, never horizontally, when it can so easily swing towards its owner's neighbour. Fatigue sometimes causes lazy behaviour, with the gun carried horizontally alongside the owner's thigh: lethal pointing. This has been seen even on a driven shoot. Between drives the best way to carry your gun is broken over your forearm, or closed over your shoulder, trigger guard uppermost, or in its sleeve.

Safety glasses, usually tinted yellow, are favoured by some people. A reasonable precaution if you do not mind wearing specs. Flak jackets are not yet the in thing on most moors.

As mentioned previously, a safety precaution adopted on many shoots is for a horn to be blown when the beaters reach a line about 100 yards from the butts; after this no shooting in front is allowed. An important point here is that Guns wearing ear mufflers sometimes do not hear the horn, and may continue to shoot in front in a dangerous manner. Protection for the ear-drums while shooting has received much sensible attention in recent years, but the method adopted, especially while shooting game as distinct from clays, should not preclude the wearer hearing normal speech, nor a warning blast on the horn. Possibly ear valves, inserted in the ear, could be safer than over-ear head-phone types.

If safety means do not shoot where you should not, remember to have a care too about the seasons, at any rate in August. 'Duck over!' calls an observant loader during a lull in a small drive on the low ground. A newcomer in the centre of the line, conscious that the approaching mallard is not in season until 1 September, lowers his gun. But it is, in fact, a blackcock, identified by someone else an instant later; so what is the date today? Blackcock are in season from 20 August, although from the sporting point of view they are usually not sought-after quarry until the end of September. Incidentally, besides their somewhat similar wing beats, blackcock can be confused with duck because of their habit of circling round high over ground they have just left.

Ricochets can also cause trouble, for shot will bounce off hard surfaces such as roads, trees and walls. On a grouse moor the biggest hazard is the presence of rocks, coupled with the high proportion of low shots. An excellent and experienced shot once fired at a grouse behind his butt at about 45° to the line of butts. There was a cry from the neighbouring butt where one of the occupants had been struck on the side of the face. Blood flowed and the Gun took the lady to a doctor, although fortunately the injury was not serious. This unfortunate accident caused pain and discomfort to the victim and the Gun, who was blameless, had to miss the rest of his day's shooting.

Ricochets off rocks pose a difficult problem. If you are in that sort of country a glance around will show the potential danger. There is not much you can do about it, except possibly to note an awkwardly placed rock and refrain from shooting in that direction. But will your neighbour exercise similar restraint? The alarming feature of ricochets is their unexpectedness, but in terms of man-hours, shots fired, distance walked and pellets per cubic 30-inch circle or some such they do not present a greater danger than, say, crossing Piccadilly in the rush hour, or hang gliding.

As well as producing quite high birds sometimes and startlingly low ones very often, driven grouse shooting frequently offers large numbers of birds all at once. These are not necessarily packs in the accepted sense, but several coveys which have joined together temporarily, perhaps feeding in an area of particularly succulent blaeberries; or in bad weather they may congregate along the top of a ridge where they can the better see the surrounding countryside. Or during a drive coveys put up separately by the beaters may alight in the same areas, short of the butts, and then all get up together as the drive progresses. When such a mass of birds comes over it needs good self-discipline to shoot calmly and methodically, picking a bird deliberately and then moving on to the next one, all in front of the butt.

As an example of how many birds may fly together a little later in the season, not long ago a Gun shot off seven barrels at one pack. He was alone in the butt and had to reload by himself, while grouse streamed over in a whicker of a myriad wings. It was a case of hurrying slowly, and efficiently.

For some people the most interesting and rewarding part of shooting lies in the dogwork. Not everyone can own a dog, especially those who have to live in cities to earn the money

Above **Right and left** As one bird falls the shooter swings onto another

Opposite above **Birds pass the butt** As the birds come up to his butt, the Gun takes one and will then turn for a shot behind, no other birds approaching from the front

Opposite below **Ricochet danger** With rocks like these close behind the butts the danger of ricochets is obvious, especially when a low bird flies between the butts

Hilly country A grouse moor where the glens have very steep sides. The shooter is changing guns as a bird flies overhead. Below him his neighbour needs to be careful about taking any birds up the hill from him which enables them to go shooting; but non-owners are usually appreciative of the help given by the dogs, although they are often unaware of the problems faced by owners.

To start with, all visiting dogs which have been having a soft time drowsing in the sun down south need sharpening up in their training, and toughening up in their physical condition. Road work is good for this and helps to harden the pads, which will have a severe time when the dog reaches the moors. One way of achieving this exercise is to let the dog trot alongside a bicycle on quiet country roads, a 'walk' of some four or five miles taking a mere half an hour.

It is important, too, that the dog should not be grossly overweight because it simply will not be able to compete with the rough, hard going, especially on a hot August day. Often visiting dogs compare most unfavourably with the hard-muscled, lean, fit dogs belonging to the keepers: dogs which take part in every drive and then do some swift picking-up between drives.

Heat and dryness make difficulties for the best dogs; when the smell of the heather flowers is so sweet and strong to us, it is amazing how the dogs can distinguish anything through it. Sometimes clouds of pollen rise from the heather and every-one's shoes are covered with it; yet somehow that magical scenting ability of the dogs still finds the game. Provided, of course, that the ground has not been fouled by a lot of people stumping up and down.

All sorts of dogs may turn up on a grouse moor, the most common being labrador retrievers and springer spaniels; black or chocolate labradors are the least conspicuous to the birds. Other breeds appear too, like cockers and curlycoats, flatcoats and perhaps even a spry little honey-coloured Tibetan spaniel, bouncing over the heather with flying furry ears and plumed tail. West Highland terriers have been known to do the best that their short legs will permit and it is not unknown for a keeper to bring his anti-poacher Alsatian; these sagacious animals, when work bred, are clever enough to learn to do most jobs, including retrieving grouse. Vizslas and other HPRs also appear, mostly in the retriever role, at which they perform as well as most. They are usually handled by grateful owners who wish to enlarge their dogs' experience, perhaps before going on to Field Trials.

Since the country is so open, the dogs' misdemeanours are obvious for all to see, and this places quite a strain on responsible owners and handlers. The blue hare often does not run very fast and neither thick heather nor obesity may prevent a wild spaniel from running in and chasing one, and catching it as well. An awkward situation for its owner as he walks with the other Guns to the butts. Worse may follow, when, for instance, during the drive one of the labradors dashes off from its place behind a butt, grabs a bird fallen behind and then lies down and starts eating it. The dog belongs to a loader and remains impervious to the poor fellow's shouts but the Gun understands; perhaps he has a doubtful dog of his own which he left at home. 'Run out and grab it,' he says. 'I won't shoot till you get back.'

On another drive one of the ladies in a butt has put her young dog on a lead, very sensibly. Halfway through, the dog slips its collar and runs to collect a bird 40 yards away. But on its way there the Gun in the next butt drops a bird just in front of the dog: it is not dead and not even a normal runner, but a flutterer; the dog grabs at it and the bird skips away, half flying and running and leading its pursuer along the line of butts. Shooting continues and dead birds are falling all around and about. The dog picks up one and starts back to its owner but on the way drops the bird to collect a different one; it is considerably confused. But what of the lady holding an empty lead? If she is the host's daughter things are not *too* awful; if she is but the fiancée of a young man asked to the shoot for the first time his future is by no means bright!

All these things and many more do happen. It can be an anguished time for all but the handler of Field Trial material. After the drive everybody, Guns, loaders, wives, etc, starts to pick up birds which are often lying in the open close to the butts, but then someone calls a friend who has a dog and says, 'I had a bird down in this area but damned if I can find it.'

So the dog owner indicates the supposed fall to his labrador which busies about using its nose, working well, covering the ground. After a couple of minutes the shooter thinks to himself,

Over the wall A big dog makes light of a big wall which might cause difficulties for a small one

Spaniel and ptarmigan A marvellous sight for the dog's owner

Labrador and runner A satisfactory end to that long search for the missing bird

'I told him the bird dropped about *here*. Why the hell does he let his perishing dog run around over *there*?' You have to be a dog owner to understand why; or to appreciate the immense pleasure which results when the errant dog suddenly stops, signals to you with its tail, 'I've got something here!' and comes galloping back with a runner in its mouth.

And here are a couple of professional pickers-up working their dogs carefully over all the area a hundred yards or more behind the butts. Each has three or four dogs, worked in turn, and probably a youngster who is out to see what goes on and who will be kept on the lead all day. The dogs look in super condition with beautiful glossy coats. Ask their handlers at the end of the day what they are fed on – it is always an interesting talking point.

The contribution of this efficient team may be as much as 10 per cent of the bag, much of it collected without the shooters even realizing that the birds were down.

Over there is old Bob, the retired keeper, methodically sending out his two in turn. This is his real joy now; he may be getting old and creaky in the joints but he can still work a dog, and he does not have to walk far. His labrador is working around with the others, while the little springer bitch keeps to heel.

'Can't understand where that bird went,' says the Gun.

'Well, Shot has searched all round where you said,' replies his wife.

'We'll put the dogs over it again,' says a picker-up.

'Let me try old Samson,' says another Gun. 'He's got a marvellous nose.'

Bob comes up to them and they all variously explain to him just how difficult it is to find this bird. Bob feels a little bump on the side of his knee. He looks down.

'This what you're lookin' for?' says the eye of the little springer bitch, and what is in her mouth but the missing bird.

The dogs meet some very varied country on the hill, most of it tougher than that in the pheasant coverts of the south. Galloping through long heather is tiring, and running over burnt heather and rocks is hard on the pads. A big dog is better than a little one because it will not tire so quickly, and can more easily cope with, for instance, the dry-stone walls of the low ground. All the same it is amazing how quite small cockers can get over these walls; and isn't it a beautiful sight when your dog tops a wall with a grouse in its mouth? Vets are apt to say that you should take care over this wall jumping because the dog may easily strain a ligament: doubtless sound medical advice but not so easy to follow. A bit like telling a Grand National jockey to be careful going over Becher's Brook in case he should break his neck.

Most moors have springs and bogs and water courses so there is usually no difficulty about the dogs getting a drink. All the same, sometimes the hill may be dry and perhaps it is known to be so in the vicinity of the lunch hut; it is always sensible to carry a bottle of water for one's dog.

A potential danger for dogs is an adder bite. It does not often happen but some years and locations occasionally produce an unusual number of these snakes. Dogs nearly always recover from a bite, although small breeds have less chance than bigger ones. If an animal is bitten, take it immediately to a vet, keeping it as quiet as possible in the meantime. If the accident happens on a Saturday afternoon, you are fifty miles from any sizeable town, and Monday is a Bank Holiday, you still have to try to get professional medical assistance with minimum delay. You can help the dog a certain amount by washing the wound thoroughly and applying a cold water compress to the limb, the idea being to reduce the circulation as much as possible.

Other people's dogs are pretty awful, aren't they? Especially in the transport, when they try to climb about on the seats, scramble over the lunch baskets in the back and fall off in a snarling heap as the car hits a rough patch. They will not sit still, but must be up and looking out of the windows, panting smelly breath at the back of your neck and dripping saliva on to your clothes. All agog, they tremble and shake, and sometimes whine, too. And there is nothing like a brisk dog fight in the back of a small Land-Rover full of men and guns. But on the way home all is peaceful; the dogs are whacked (metaphorically!), quite content to flop down anywhere in an amicable heap, caring nothing for anything but the chance of a quick kip.

The dog fight in a car can be a bore. Often it is started by the first dog to leap aboard who may or may not belong to the car's owner. It makes a grab at the next one in and, having the double military advantages of surprise and a commanding height, it is likely to achieve a successful initial thrust, and possibly a blood-spilling grip. Damage is unlikely to be severe but unfortunately the torn ear or leg may require a swift withdrawal from the scene of battle, and a visit to the vet's for stitching, and possibly a penicillin injection.

It is a reasonable precaution to be wary about encouraging a dog to jump into a vehicle already containing one other dog; the likelihood of a battle could depend on the sexes of the animals and whether the first one aboard belongs to the owner of the vehicle. As an antidote for an unexpected bite, and for other injuries such as wounds from barbed wire or broken glass, some dog owners keep in their car an emergency supply of aureomycin powder.

Another possible danger to gundogs, more especially on the lower ground, is slug pellets, which may prove fatal if eaten. Modern farming methods encourage spraying before direct drilling with a consequent reduction of weeds; this means slugs can feed directly on the young corn, so the farmer puts down poison for them. It is usually in the form of metaldehyde or draza pellets, which are dog killers. If a careless tractor driver leaves a pile of pellets spilled out of a bag, or even an open bag on the floor of a barn, a dog may come across them, and guzzle them. It will soon begin to twitch and salivate, and then go into spasms. If it can be made to vomit, its life may be saved. One way of achieving this is to force some washing soda down its throat as quickly as possible. And so it is a good idea to carry a small packet of soda, either in crystal or powder form. Slug pellets are highly unlikely to be found on a grouse moor but dogs could pick them up on lower agricultural land, possibly at the morning's meeting place. One cannot take precautions against every conceivable mishap, with pockets full of potions and lotions and a sprig of laurel to ward off lightning, but dire things do happen to dogs and sometimes it is worth carrying, at least in the car, some first-aid antidotes.

Swallowing a wasp can cause a considerable shock to a dog's

nervous system and, as always, the stock remedy is to get the animal to the vet quickly, where it may well require heart supportive therapy. The trouble usually starts when the dog bites at angry wasps embedded in its fur after passing close to a nest.

There are many stories concerning the understanding and perspicacity of dogs. Conrad Lorenz, author of *King Solomon's Ring* and *Man meets Dog*, has described the uncanny ability of a dog not so much to understand words, or even sentences, as to realize the implication of their sounds. This can apply to circus animals, but a countryman thinks more of a working dog.

Charles St John tells of visiting the cottage of a shepherd whose dog had the extra job of guarding its master's small plots of oats and potatoes. In the course of conversation, and as a demonstration to St John, the shepherd casually said, 'I think the cow is in the potatoes.'

Immediately the dog, previously apparently asleep at its master's feet, got up and jumped out of the open window. It then climbed up the low turf roof and looked toward the potato field: no cow. The dog came down and went to look in the byre: cow there. So it jumped back into the room, gave its master a mildly reproachful look, and went back to sleep.

Exciting as grouse shooting undoubtedly is, the picture of the day can never be complete without the dogs. As well as their marvellous achievements during a shoot, some mysterious failures also occur. One of these concerns the towered bird which falls in the open, on quite short grass and visible from the height of a man's eye 20 yards away. And yet the dogs cannot find it. Such a bird has probably been hit by only one pellet and falls with no drift of feathers to help a searching dog, and no blood wound. The apparent absence of scent seems to baffle even the Field Trial champions, which of course does not always entirely displease owners of humbler dogs who cannot help being that little bit jealous of the normal urbane efficiency of the super dogs!

The training of gundogs is a long and expensive process demanding great patience. Expert advice and assistance is needed. It always seems curious that people who want to ski or play bridge or golf are usually prepared to take lessons; whereas

A walk to the butts The butts can be seen diagonally across the top of the picture. The Guns had to walk down and up the hill to them and, on their way back, have still another 300 yards or so to go before they reach the transport

for more important things like rearing children or training a dog they think they know it all and do not bother to ask for any help or even advice.

Grouse shooting can be a strenuous business. Walking-up is the hardest work; dogging does not require quite so much effort to find the birds because the dogs do it for you. Driving can be very lazy for the Guns, especially as sometimes return drives over the same line of butts all day can mean they need walk only a few hundred yards to and from the transport. But it is not always so. There may be a long steep walk up to each line of butts throughout the day, and even walking downhill can stretch flabby calf muscles unaccustomed to moving far without mechanical aid. That walking, however, is easy compared with the disciplined walking of keeping in line and being prepared to shoot.

An unusual form of shooting was described by Abel Chapman, the sportsman-naturalist of 100 years ago. This involved walking, but in company with a horse and cart which acted the part of the classic stalking horse first described in shooting literature by Gervase Markham in 1621. The Gun kept behind the keeper leading the horse, and together they carefully drew closer to the birds, not directly at them but on a curving course. The sport took place in October and November when grouse had become too wild to approach in the normal way. Much of the skill of this method lay in seeing the birds in the first place: that extraordinary ability of all stalkers which never fails to impress the beginner, who at first can see no sign of the bird or beast being pursued.

Picking-up was left until the end of the manoeuvres, the dog meanwhile being tethered underneath the cart. Occasionally a bird, having unwittingly allowed the cart to approach a little closer than intended, would squat as close as possible to the ground rather than fly; the curious word used for this behaviour was to 'scrogg'. It seems most improbable that this sport of 'carting' has been pursued since the turn of the century; if carried out today with a Land-Rover it just might have some success but because of what even Chapman called its 'unsportsmanlike advantage' it would be labelled poaching.

When the day's shooting is over and the bag has been laid out and counted, and the grouse sorted into young and old, the paid hands get their wages. The keeper must then hang up the birds in the game larder, which needs to be cool and airy and preferably fly proof. A few squirts with a fly-killer spray is a help too; keeping the game in good condition until the dealer comes to collect it needs that little more trouble than caring for a bag of pheasants in November. The day's shooting is not really finished until the bag is properly checked and stored.

Shooting driven grouse is a unique challenge. What might be considered a high bird when pheasant shooting is one of the easier grouse shots. So often the birds suddenly materialize out of the void, low, slanting across the butt line, rising a little, falling, veering, jinking; you have to stand up to them and watch very closely, like facing a really fast Test Match bowler at cricket or taking on a World Tennis Association ace server. Experience helps enormously, and it is not quite so terrifying after the first few times.

Remarkable bags have been made over the years. Here are some of the best:

Recorded on a tombstone in the churchyard at Bewcastle, Cumberland: 'Jonathan Telford . . . was one of the best moor game shooters in the North of England in the time of his shooting he bagged 59 grouse in seven double shots.'

1860 Cannock Chase, Staffordshire	252 blackgame in one day.
1861 Drumlanrig, Dumfriesshire	247 blackgame in one day, and 1586 in the season.
1866 Achnashellach, Ross-shire	122 ptarmigan to one Gun, Hon Geoffrey Hill, in one day.
1871 Grandtully Castle, Perthshire	440 grouse in one day, over dogs, to one Gun, Maharajah Duleep Singh, riding a pony.
1872 Wemmergill, Yorkshire	2000 grouse in one day, 17,064 in the season.
1872 Dalnaspidal, Perthshire	Four Guns, over dogs, in four days bagged 2856 grouse; best day 870.
1872 High Force, Co. Durham	Eight Guns over nineteen

	days shot 15,484 grouse.
1872 Bolton Abbey, Yorkshire	More than 15,000 grouse in the season.
1872 Wemmergill, Yorkshire	Sir Frederick Milbank, at a driven shoot, had 728 grouse to his own gun, out of a day's bag of 2070. That season he shot 18,231 birds.
1887 Hunt Hill, Angus	Captain W. H. Tomasson, shot 458 grouse in one day, over dogs.
1888 Blubberhouses, Yorkshire	Lord Walsingham, in one long day of twenty drives, himself shot 1070 grouse.
1905 Moy Hall, Inverness-shire	1828 grouse in one day; 14,254 in the season.
1911 Roan Fell, Dumfriesshire	2523 grouse in one day.
1915 Littledale and Abbeystead, Lancashire	2929 grouse in one day.
1931 Glendye, Kincardineshire	955 grouse in one day.
1934 Wemmergill, Yorkshire	2697 grouse in one day.
1982 Co. Durham	Nine visitors from abroad shot 1009 grouse in three days.

Such large bags of grouse are unlikely to be made again, apart from the last one; it is true to say, however, that in a good year several of the big estates still succeed in making bags of 10,000 birds. If the high numbers cause any slight feeling of revulsion it is well to consider a line of thought expressed by the American wildlife writer, Fred P. Evenden: 'Most non-endangered wildlife species are somewhat like an apple tree. You do not ruin the tree by picking its fruit, nor do you help it by allowing the apples to fall to the ground and rot.'

7 Problems and Paradoxes

Dear Sir,
    One of your party Shot my Dog on Friday the 18th current on the moor opeside the Farm of Dallah and they likewise burried the Dog in a peat moss in preasence of witnesses.
    Please send me £3 as the value of the Dog within six days if not settled within this Specified time I must take prosedings for the value of my Dog.
    Yours truly,
    James Gunn
    Dallah, Glenvellet.

That letter, written in 1882 and reproduced here with changes of name and place, is an early example of the sort of thing with which the owner of a grouse moor may have to contend.

More complex and more expensive vexations, however, can appear on the word-processing screen of today's owner, agent or tenant. Bypassing supply and demand conundrums concerning quantities – for example the number of bottles of Bourbon required by the boozers, or claret by the Countesses – the owner who lets his shooting has to consider all manner of complaints. From interference with domestic arrangements to grievances about the size of the bag, the variety of headaches that come his way is almost endless; although at least today's agent is unlikely to receive from the family renting one of his moors the complaint, 'You never told us that our footman and butler would have to *share* a room!'

Some grumbles from paying guests can be quite petty, as when cartridges are supplied and their cost added on to the bill. Then niggles sometimes arise: 'I'm sure I didn't use as many cartridges as *that*. I bet the keeper is taking them for himself.'

Experienced owners try to avoid such arguments by having a flat rate for cartridges, and similarly by standardizing other extras such as tips for loaders.

The main worry for an owner running a commercial shoot arises when inexperienced visitors object to being told what to do: 'I'm on holiday, I don't want to be pushed around.' And the implication is, 'I'm spending a lot of money on this trip, I expect a good bag, and I do not like being hustled if I want to take my time and gossip with my friends.'

In fact, generally the paying visitors become good friends of the owner and frequently return year after year. Which brings us to another of the owner's problems: how can he continue to pay the exorbitant and increasing local rates he is charged, without putting up his prices so much that they frighten away the customers? This situation is aggravated in a bad year, when shooting is curtailed or even cancelled, and the rating authority's charges are based on an average bag over five years.

Would-be shooters have problems too; the first is to find the shooting. In default of having the right friends, who will ask you as a guest, you have to seek it on a paying basis; some agencies who specialize in providing grouse shooting are listed in Appendix A. It is important for the client to be clear about what he can expect for his money: some lettings are on the house-party basis, with all drinks included, in a comfortable lodge where dinner is served by footmen against a background of crested silver and ancestral oil paintings. Accommodation may, on the other hand, be in a hotel with arrangements being made by the client.

The important point about booking through agencies is that they are experienced in the problems of both shoot owner and paying guest, and will include in the contract some form of insurance against deliberate default or unavoidable cancellation by either side.

Letting prices are reduced later in the season, when bags will usually be smaller. In a bumper year, though, the owner may have some difficulty in finding enough good Guns in October to shoot his abundance of grouse. Beaters are also scarce then, but at least less of them are needed than earlier on, because the birds will have become wilder and more easily moved. As with many sports and pastimes nowadays, grouse shooting can be obtained more cheaply by anyone prepared to do so in what the holiday brochures call the low season.

Shooting rents are decided by a generally accepted rate against the expected bag. Thus at £20 a brace, a day on which fifty brace of birds is expected would cost the Guns £1000. Rates in 1986 varied from about £45 a brace in August down to about £15 in October, for driven birds; walking-up charges are about half.

Letting shooting is by no means new, although a hundred years or more ago a moor was usually let for a season or several seasons. Letting by the week or by the day is a more recent feature, as is the increased interest by foreign visitors. Americans, if not always madly enthusiastic about accommodation arrangements, have for a long time been eager to come for the shooting. Game records dated 1914 refer to letting to visitors from New York a 'most luxurious shooting lodge' *with* bathrooms. That final 's' is quite a surprise.

The friendly enthusiasm of American shooting visitors sparkles in their letters when they get home. For example, 'Don't forget the many sportsmen in the USA who have taken their guns to your country, loved every minute of it and cannot stop dreaming about the day of another return.'

This applies to practically all the other foreign sportsmen too, except the unhappy few who have experienced a shortage of birds and consequently consider they have not received their money's worth. Unfortunately, grouse shooting is always somewhat unpredictable as far as numbers go, for a variety of reasons mentioned earlier. This is in contrast to pheasant shooting where, except in cases of excessively poor marksmanship, the renting price of a day can be directly related to the number of birds actually shot.

Anyone on a grouse shoot, but not actively participating, will witness from time to time some rather curious behaviour in and around the butts. Such an observer could be the owner or shoot manager, hoping that all goes well for his guests but not carrying a gun himself; without *that* responsibility he can see the funny side of the things people do. Such as:

Put on sun-tan lotion.
Read a novel.

Strain their eyes staring in front for half an hour, and then wipe away the tears with a large handkerchief just as the birds come over.

Embroidery or knitting; usually by ladies just behind the butt.

Set the butt on fire with the end of cigarettes lit to keep the midges at bay.

Drink a can of beer, or maybe two, purloined from the lunch basket.

Stand upright in a cream shirt, wearing no tie and no hat.

Take off waistcoat, jersey, jacket, with much button fiddling and sleeve and zip pulling.

Put on ditto.

Light pipe, head well down to avoid the wind.

Natter loudly and endlessly, boring their companion and alarming the birds.

Fall asleep.

Light a fire, because it is cold in October.

Intervene when child plays with Dinky toys, sheep turds, cartridges or the dog.

Fail to intervene when child plays with Dinky toys, etc, until it is too late.

Urinate.

Naturally, many of these actions take place as the birds arrive, and sometimes just outside the butt, where they spoil what might have been a good photograph.

One of the odd problems about grouse matters is that the more you read or ask questions the more contrary opinions you will find – and quite often flat contradictions, even among the experts. Capercailzie crashing out of woodland are described by enthusiastic shooters, thrilled to have had the opportunity to bag one of these comparatively rare birds; and then an authority writing about them stresses their silence. Everyone enjoys seeing red deer on the high hill, a fine sight and an added interest to the day; but the keeper says they are an abomination: they eat the grouse eggs, d'ye ken? Incidentally, stalkers sometimes do not like grouse because they can spoil a stalk by suddenly taking wing and alerting the stags.

You cannot rear grouse, people say, the birds are all wild.

That is true, referring to the ones you shoot; but they *can* be reared in pens, fed on pheasant food with no supplementary quartz grit, and they will lay and bring up broods. The difficulty about rearing them to shoot lies in their failure to adapt to the chosen release ground. Reared birds can even thrive without heather, and they are easily tamed. A cock kept around garden or yard on the 'free range' principle becomes splendidly pugnacious in the breeding season and is quite capable of seeing off the house dogs. Such a tame cock kept in appropriate country will find a mate nearby, guard the nest and his brood most fiercely, and later return to his owner. The point about which there should be no controversy is that grouse are *not* artificially implanted on noblemen's moors for plutocrats to slay, whatever the papers may say.

'Nothing is so easy to shoot as a grouse,' is a quote from a book. It is qualified considerably when you realize that the writer means only the type of bird which he has experienced, walking-up at the beginning of the season and methodically knocking down every member of any covey found. Driven birds, especially in September or October, are more likely to merit the accolade of being the most difficult to shoot.

According to one authority it is most important to kill off old cocks at the end of the season. But another source says, 'Nonsense, quite unnecessary, especially on a driving moor, and anyway it is not possible to be certain which are the old and which the young ones by November.'

'Nearly all butts are made of turf,' says one. 'Grouse butts should always be made of stones,' says another. Obviously such firm statements must emanate from a source just a little too hidebound by the circumstances in his own locality. The wandering Gun, however, chances on many solutions to a whole series of difficult questions and from them and his game book arise a multitude of memories.

Memories of shooting days, this day just over, and some of the others back through the years – so many different characteristics come to mind: the high hills of Perthshire, stretching away, ridge after ridge, purple and cloud-shadowed for fifteen or twenty miles; and below this line of high butts, 1500 feet below them, runs the long, blue, curving shape of Loch Tummel.

That keen young visitor from overseas went out in front of his butt as soon as the Guns began taking their places, and carefully set up a bit of stick among the heather as a 40-yard range mark. He was so eager to do his best, and that it should be good enough. But when the birds came they were so low and fast he scarcely fired a shot. He was not the only one to find them difficult.

Then there was that 10-foot-deep ravine in Co. Durham, monsoon-like rain, and a peaty bank in front of the Guns, who were standing halfway up the side, with a scurrying stream below them. Grass and rushes behind, and mud underfoot, absurdly difficult to find a steady platform. Rain dripped off the brim of your hat, and you did not dare to hold the gun muzzles up in case it filled with water; the dog looked reproachfully miserable. And then hundreds of birds poured over: incredible shooting, amazing really that anyone could stand up steadily enough to swing a gun properly. But they all did, and it was a record bag for that drive.

A ghyll in Cumbria, a steep gulley, or could it have been a combe or goyle, a wadi or what? Anyway, it was all green, no heather in sight, although there must have been some all around as, indeed, you saw after the drive. But to start with everything seemed so different from Scotland; no butts, just a numbered post. Someone hidden out in front of the Guns, where no one could see him, gave a toot on a horn when grouse were approaching. Invaluable. Can't think how one would have coped without him.

Extraordinary how *good* the good shots were. And maddeningly effortless. A young man, son of the host – so his casual slacks-and-golf-jacket turn-out was beyond reproach – almost never missed. His shooting style was terrible but his good looks and long blond hair made him seem like a film star. So nonchalant, he made it look really easy; and so charming to everyone. One blessed by the gods.

And then the low ground, quite unlike the tops. Flat country, even though it is in the Highlands, and grassy, ordinary pasture fields with cattle or sheep. But ditches cut through the peat, and above ground, fence-type butts. Scots pines in the background and a chance of blackcock, they said. The rust-coloured trunks and the windswept branches, handsome trees whose shoots and seeds make popular eating for black grouse. And the excitement when somebody does get a blackcock, his first, and has his photograph taken holding it, with that funny grin on his face which is so difficult to suppress, like an angler with a big fish. Different journeys up on to the moor, the convoys of Land-Rovers and sometimes big open-backed lorries; occasionally a comfortable real car but one with special performance features, like a Citroën or Subaru. And the sturdy Range Rovers whose calm, upright-sitting passengers often seem to be skimming effortlessly along like people in a railway carriage; with their dogs neatly in the rear compartment they are all somehow on a higher plane than those in humbler transport. Everyone watches with some apprehension as the driver in front is confronted by a small plank bridge over a torrent of brown, shining peaty water; it looks at least 6 inches narrower than the track of whatever is approaching it. Miraculously, all vehicles cross.

There have been visits on other occasions, too. In the spring when the birds are paired and the cock looks so specially handsome with his big red wattle. In the harsh, hard times of winter when the hills seem to the visitor more conducive to ski-ing. And in the summer, early in the morning long before the other shooters have woken. Then the birds come down to the roads to pick up grit; they sit on walls as a thundering lorry hurtles past, and walk casually along the verges showing a nearly disdainful tameness towards man and his works. But even while most of the birds are relaxed a sentinel remains, alert and wary, looking all round, and up, for possible danger.

Memories of bygone times will inevitably include several conflicting opinions on so many matters and the varied advice given on them. It must be admitted that some of the advice in this book is a counsel of perfection. People *do* chatter in butts, and flankers rarely number more than three or four, even if the theoretical best number might be ten. And many good shots are quite unaware of the boring of their guns. Ask one, a wise and clever fellow whom you have just seen kill nineteen grouse out of twenty-four shots; with a cheerful grin he replies, 'No idea!'

One of today's best ten game shots uses an under-and-over gun, and a foreign one at that. Ask him about its boring and he says, 'Oh, just standard.' The seeker after truth wants to know about the cartridges used by this magic-man (and if you watch him shoot you will think Gandalf at least, and perhaps Merlin as well, is guiding his shot); how big a load, and what size shot, and what *make*? 'Well,' he says, 'One ounce of shot is enough, especially when you get a bit older; I generally use 7s, buy them by the thousand, take whatever's going. Cheaper that way.' And although the 12-bore is the standard game gun, many people, who are often very good shots, use 16- and 20-bore.

There are really no universal *rules* about grouse shooting, except those concerned with safety. People *do* stamp around the butts area looking for birds after a drive, regardless of suggested codes of behaviour; they do sometimes interfere with the dogs, because the man smell is stronger than the bird smell, but nothing will ever stop them doing it. And some of those 'Things People Do' mentioned earlier in this chapter may not really be so heinous; after all, if the beaters are still on their way out and there is no likelihood of birds appearing for twenty minutes at least, why shouldn't a Gun sit down and read his newspaper? Like Drake playing bowls before dealing with the Armada.

We have to do a little debunking of the prelates of exactitude. Ordinary mortals simply do not behave as some of the rule-makers would have them. See there, lying on the grass outside the butt, the pretty blonde wife in her purple knickerbockers. She also wears a blue jacket, pink-striped shirt and no hat, and is accompanied by a red dachshund. (Incidentally, she also makes the most marvellous North Country fruit cake, scrumptious with cheese at a shooting lunch.) Could there be any more startling colours likely to 'turn the birds', as that old cur-mudgeon phrased it, when grumbling about the presence of ladies on the moor? Perhaps she is just sensible about sitting still, or else grouse are colour blind; the fact is that her husband shot seventeen birds on that drive with not the slightest concern about them jinking away from his butt.

Another paradox arises because economic necessity forces nearly all owners of grouse moors to let some of their shooting, by the day or week, or even season. Expenses are staggering: £20,000 a year in rates, for instance. How many people are employed, and paid, by an owner on one grouse shooting day?

Thirty beaters, five keepers, six flankers, four pickers-up, eight loaders, two gamecart men, five drivers, a total of sixty. With lunch for the Guns, a few overheads and the price of petrol, this can mount up to a cost of £1000 and often more.

Commercialism, says the dedicated and knowledgeable keeper, is the worst thing for the birds. Granted that his employer must raise the cash to keep the estate going, he is appalled at the idea that rigid plans might be made concerning one of Nature's more problematical and unpredictable creatures. You should never, he says, decide to shoot this beat on Monday and that one on Tuesday and such-and-such on Wednesday. Where you go is best determined by the state of the weather, particularly the wind, on the morning in question. Even the habit of the same guests coming on the same dates each year is bad, he thinks; and when it is a poor year their visit should be cancelled. Luckily, he does not have to work out the estate's accounts.

If commercialism might be bad for the birds it may also be the only saviour of the estate. And only by the continuation of grouse shooting, and pheasant and partridge shooting, fox hunting, stag hunting, beagling, coursing, stalking and all forms of river and lake angling, will the continuation of the species be assured. Of them all, the grouse has a peculiar charm, upstaging high pheasants, big salmon and all the others.

Much is now known about the grouse; it is no longer quite the bird of mystery that it was. Nevertheless, it remains a bird that provokes some misunderstanding – although there should not be anything mythical about the manner in which it is shot – and to some moor owners it remains an ungrateful bird, because it flies away or dies, however much they do for it!

One thing is certain: the grouse's whole life is geared to avoidance of predators, and of them all, man-with-a-gun is the least harmful.

Appendix A

Agencies which can Arrange Shooting

Avon and Airlie Game Farms, Avon, Chippenham, Wiltshire (Paddy Fetherston-Godley).

Sportselect, Great Edstone House, Kirkbymoorside, Yorkshire (Kit Egerton and James Holt).

Strutt and Parker, 13 Hill Street, Berkeley Square, London W1X 8DL.

Macsport, 68 Station Road, Banchory, Kincardineshire AB3 3YJ.

Parkmore Sporting Estates, Parkmore House, Dufftown, Banffshire AB5 4DL (John Brockbank).

Peter Readman Sporting Agency, Hirsel Law, Guards Road, Coldstream, Berwickshire TD12 4HX.

Cowley and Fell Sporting Agency, Cree Cottage, Woodland Head, Yeaford, Crediton, Devon.

Smiths Gore, 26 Coniscliffe Road, Darlington DL3 7JX; 12 Little College Street, London SW1P 3SH.

Brackenbank Lodge, Lazonby, Penrith, Cumbria (R. N. Burton).

Savills, 14 Skeldergate, York; 20 Grosvenor Hill, Berkeley Square, London W1X OHQ.

John Birth Sporting Organization, Greenlawalls Lodge, Duddo, Berwick on Tweed TD15 2PR.

A and C Sporting Services, Hornby Castle Estate Office, Hornby, Lancaster.

Major Neil Ramsay, Farleyer, Aberfeldy, Perthshire PH15 2JE.

Kylnadrochit Lodge, Tomintoul, Banffshire AB3 9HJ (T. van Holten).

Davis and Bowring, 6 Main Street, Kirkby Lonsdale, Carnforth, Lancashire LA6 2AF.

David Patmore, 20 Stonegate, York.

Appendix B

Organizations Concerned with Grouse and Shooting

1 The Game Conservancy. Secretary: H. Smith-Carington, Fordingbridge, Hampshire SP6 1EF.
   Carries out scientific research and practical investigation into game, its habitat and the improvement of shoots.
2 North of England Grouse Research Project, c/o The Game Conservancy. Chairman: The Earl Peel, Gunnerside Estate Office, 8 Main Street, Kirkby Lonsdale, Carnforth, Lancashire LA6 2AF.
   Investigates the factors influencing grouse bags and the practical ways of improving stocks.
3 Institute of Terrestrial Ecology, Hill of Brathens, Glassel, Banchory, Kincardineshire AB3 4BY.
   The Grouse and Moorland Ecology Group studies the population and management of grouse and moorland, under Dr Adam Watson.
4 The British Association for Shooting and Conservation. Director: Lt Cdr J. W. Anderton, Marford Mill, Rossett, Clwyd LL12 0HL.
   Has many affiliated local clubs whose members it helps with advice and information on all aspects of shooting.
5 The British Field Sports Society. Director: John Hopkinson, 59 Kennington Road, London SE1 7PZ.
   Looks after all field sports, particularly combating propaganda opposed to them.

6 *Shooting Times and Country Magazine*, 10 Sheet Street, Windsor, Berkshire SL4 1BG.
   Reports on game shooting and carries advertisements for shoots, hotels, dogs, guns and shooting schools.

7 *The Field*, Carmelite House, Carmelite Street, London EC4 0JA.
   Articles and advertisements on all country sports and equipment.

8 The British Shooting Sports Council. Secretary: P. A. Gouldsbury, Pentridge, Salisbury, Wiltshire SP5 5QX.
   Promotes and safeguards the lawful use of sporting guns, and represents the views of members concerned with the manufacture of firearms.

9 The Shooting Sports Trust, 22 Park Gate Road, Cannock Wood, Rugeley WS15 4RN.
   Members are traders in guns, ammunition and equipment, devoted to fighting new legislation against the interests of shooting.

10 The Campaign for Country Sports. Chairman: Humphrey Atkins. Secretary: H. J. B. Rice, Welbeck House, High Street, Guildford, Surrey GU1 3JF.
   Its objects are a) to publicize the true facts about country sports; b) to combat those organizations which try to prevent the sports, harass participants and persuade political parties to pass laws banning them; c) to preserve the freedom of the individual to choose whether to take part in field sports or not.

Appendix C

Bibliography

Shooting (Moor and Marsh), The Badminton Library, Lord
  Walsingham and Sir Ralph Payne-Gallwey, Longmans,
  Green, 1886.
Bird Life of the Borders, Abel Chapman, Gurney and Jackson,
  1889.
The Wild Sports and Natural History of the Highlands, Charles St
  John, John Murray, 1893.
Game Birds and Shooting Sketches, J. G. Millais, Henry Sotheran,
  1894.
The Grouse, Fur and Feather series, H. A. Macpherson, A. J.
  Stuart-Wortley and G. Saintsbury, Longmans, Green,
  1894.
A Sporting Tour, Col T. Thornton, Edward Arnold, 1896.
Grouse and Grouse Moors, George Malcolm and Aylmer
  Maxwell, A. & C. Black, 1910.
The Grouse in Health and Disease, Report of the Committee of
  Inquiry on Grouse Disease, Smith, Elder and Co, 1911.
The Keeper's Book, P. J. Mackie, McCorquodale, 1917.
The Natural History of Sport in Scotland with Rod and Gun, Tom
  Speedy, William Blackwood and Sons, 1920.
Shooting by Moor Field and Shore, Lonsdale Library, Seeley
  Service, 1929.
Record Bags and Shooting Records, Hugh Gladstone, Witherby,
  1930.
Grouse Shooting and Moor Management, Bernard Cazenove,
  Country Life, 1936.

Grouse Land and the Fringe of the Moor, Lord George Scott, Witherby, 1937.

The Lonsdale Keeper's Book, Lonsdale Library, Seeley Service, 1938.

Grouse Shooting, Martin Stephens, A. & C. Black, 1939.

British Game, Brian Vesey-Fitzgerald, Collins, 1946.

Elements of Shooting, Eric Parker, The Field, 1948.

Grouse – Shooting and Moor Management, Richard Waddington, Faber and Faber, 1958.

The Shotgun, T. D. S. Purdey and J. A. Purdey, A. and C. Black, 1962.

Grouse Shooting, J. K. Stanford, Percival Marshall, 1963.

The Twelfth and After, J. K. Stanford, Faber & Faber, 1964.

The Highlands and Islands, F. Fraser Darling and J. Morton Boyd, Collins, The Fontana New Naturalist, 1971.

Training Pointers and Setters for Field Trials, Professor Beazley, Alf Manners, Arnold White Robinson, 1973.

Gundogs in Britain, Edited by Tony Jackson, Barrie & Jenkins, 1974.

The Complete Book of Game Conservation, Edited by Charles Coles, Third revised edition, Stanley Paul, 1984.

The Big Shots, J. G. Rutter, Debrett-Viking Press, 1977.

Birds of Britain and Europe, Heinzel, Fitter and Parslow, Collins, 1977.

The Moorland Gamekeeper, J. Spottiswoode, David & Charles, 1977.

Border Reflections, Lord Home of the Hirsel, Collins, 1979.

Going to the Moors, Ronald Eden, John Murray, 1979.

Game and the English Landscape, Anthony Vandervell and Charles Coles, Debrett's Peerage, 1980.

Shotgun Marksmanship, Percy Stanbury and G. L. Carlisle, Fourth edition, Stanley Paul, 1980.

Shotguns and Shooting, Tony Jackson, Ward Lock, 1982.

Appendix D

Shooting Schools with Simulated Grouse

West Yorkshire Shooting Ground, Knaresborough Forest, Harrogate, Yorkshire.
Beamsley Estate Shooting School, Bolton Abbey, Yorkshire.
The Shooting Lodge, Kelbrook Manor, Kelbrook, Lancashire.
Midland Counties Shooting Grounds, Oak Edge, Wolsley Bridge, Rugeley, Staffordshire.
The Mill Shooting Grounds, Old Bolingbroke, Spilsby, Lincolnshire.
Mid-Norfolk Shooting School, Deighton Hills, Taverham, Norwich, Norfolk.
West London Shooting Grounds, Northolt, Middlesex.
Holland and Holland Shooting Grounds, Ducks Hill Road, Northwood, Middlesex.
Rogers Shooting School, Beeches Farm, Edenbridge, Kent.
Newland Hall Shooting Ground, Roxwell, Chelmsford, Essex.
Apsley Shooting Grounds, Apsley Estate, Andover, Hampshire.
Lower Lake Shooting Ground, Upton Cross, Liskeard, Cornwall.

Appendix E

Game Seasons

Shooting Seasons (England, Scotland and Wales)
As at September 1982 (all dates inclusive)

Grouse	12 August–10 December
Partridges	1 September–1 February
Pheasant	1 October–1 February
Ptarmigan	12 August–10 December
Blackgame	20 August–10 December
Capercailzie	1 October–31 January
Snipe	12 August–31 January
Woodcock	1 October–31 January
Scotland:	1 September–31 January
Hares	No close season

Wild geese and duck

Geese: Pinkfooted – Greylag – Canada – Whitefronted (England and Wales only)

Duck: Mallard – Wigeon – Teal – Pintail – Common Pochard – Tufted – Shoveler – Gadwall – Goldeneye

In or over any area below HWM of Ordinary Spring Tides	1 September–20 February
Elsewhere: The only wader that may be shot is Golden Plover	1 September–31 January
Coot and Moorhen	1 September–31 January

Shooting on Sundays may be restricted and the onus is on the individual to ascertain the exact position in each county.

Deer Seasons

SPECIES	SEX	ENGLAND AND WALES	SCOTLAND
Red	Stags	1 Aug.–30 Apr.	1 July–20 Oct.
	Hinds	1 Nov.–28 Feb.	21 Oct.–15 Feb.
Fallow	Buck	1 Aug.–30 Apr.	1 Aug.–30 Apr.
	Doe	1 Nov.–28 Feb.	21 Oct.–15 Feb.
Roe	Buck	1 Apr.–31 Oct.	1 May–20 Oct.
	Doe	1 Nov.–28 Feb.	21 Oct.–28 Feb.
Sika	Stags	1 Aug.–30 Apr.	1 Aug.–30 Apr.
	Hinds	1 Nov.–28 Feb.	21 Oct.–15 Feb.

Appendix F

A Grouse Counting System
described by Kenneth Wilson, head keeper at Leadhills, Lanarkshire

HISTORY

The following system of grouse counting began in 1956 on a very small scale and was, for experimental purposes, carried out on a small area of the moor. Over a period of years the count figures were compared with the number of grouse shot for the season on the experimental area. After a period of trial and error and many changes in the method of counting, the two sets of figures began to compare favourably.

In 1966, the system, which was by now giving worthwhile comparisons on the experimental area, was applied to the rest of the moor and the figures and predictions made known to the moor owner. The grouse count figures nowadays are eagerly awaited each year and are of great interest and value to management, shooting tenants and keepers alike because the spring count of breeding stock is an early indication; and the end-of-season total bag prediction, which the July count gives, has proved to be consistently close to the actual bag obtained in the ensuing season.

THE SYSTEM

This is made up of two counts:
1. The Breeding Stock Count done in March ('The March Count')
2. The Total Grouse Count done in July ('The July Count')

THE MARCH COUNT

Ideally, this count should be done during mid-March and should be completed by the end of the month. It is very difficult to get an accurate count in April as grouse by that time become very quiet and secretive and are difficult to put on the wing. The March Count is carried out over a number of sample areas of approximately 100 acres each. The areas are carefully chosen so that they are representative of the moors as a whole – the different altitudes, the different exposures and the different types of habitat. Habitat variations on most moors include: heather predominant; mixture of heather and grass; mixture of heather and bog cotton; grass predominant, etc.

The chosen areas or sample plots are hunted out completely by the use of dogs. Great care should be exercised in order that grouse are not counted twice. The wind can be of great help in clearing from the chosen area the grouse which have already been disturbed and counted. Leadhills Grouse Moor extends to some 12,000 acres. Fourteen areas of 100 acres each have been selected from the moor, and the same areas are counted every year, which gives a complete and accurate count over 1400 acres which are representative of the whole moor. Careful selection initially of the areas to be counted is very important in order to achieve accuracy. Cock grouse sometimes have two or even three mates, and if these are encountered they are noted. Finally the overall grouse breeding stock for the whole moor is estimated from the actual numbers counted in the sample plots. This may be expressed as a breeding hen per — acres. A breeding hen per 5 acres may be considered a high breeding stock. In Scotland the average stock density is probably of the order of a breeding hen per 10 acres.

Counting should not be attempted immediately after a prolonged period of lying snow. Snow upsets the territorial behaviour of grouse, causing them to form into groups or packs. When the snow has gone it may take a few days for the birds to break up and resume their territories. Observations over a period of years by the Grouse Research Unit have proved this. Therefore a period of three to four days after a thaw of lying snow should be allowed to pass before counting begins.

Sadly, however, it has to be admitted that if adverse conditions prevail after the stock has been counted (e.g. frosting of heather or late snowfalls or floods or rain at hatching time, etc) a high breeding stock in March will not necessarily mean a large stock of grouse at shooting time. Nevertheless it is a very useful early indicator of the state of affairs on the moor.

THE JULY COUNT

This count, the object of which is to estimate the overall grouse population just before the start of the season, is carried out in a completely different way from the March Count. The moor has to be sampled again but in our experience the March Count method of using 100-acre sample plots does not give an accurate account of grouse numbers in July because it has been found that in most years some areas will have bred differently from others, for various reasons.

The chances of obtaining inaccurate figures using the March Count sampling method is indeed great as we experienced during our experimental period.

It is impossible to count grouse over every acre on a large moor. Therefore, some alternative system had to be devised. After hard work and many errors in the early years we found that the following method has proved to be very reliable.

The most suitable way to sample any moor for this grouse count is to sample the area of the individual grouse drives plus any other areas which may be shot over by walking parties over the driving ground. Each drive is walked by the keeper with his dogs hunting the ground in as straight a line as possible from where the drive begins to the butts, arriving at, for example butt number 3. A return line or beat is taken from, for example, butt number 7 on the same drive back to the beginning again, arriving at an appropriate spot in relation to butt number 7. In other words a beat is taken through the lower part of the drive, returning on the upper part or vice versa.

Where to go counting on any particular day is dependent on the direction of the wind, which is used where possible to clear the counted grouse away from the selected line being hunted. Sometimes, and especially when grouse are plentiful, the disturbed coveys will settle again further along the selected line. Great care must be exercised so that those coveys are not counted twice. To avoid this, a deviation from the original line of advance may be required, and this should always be made towards the outer edge of the drive or area which is being counted. It will be found when grouse are in large numbers that many coveys will be put on the wing, be counted and re-settle ahead, and to try to continue on the selected or deviated route would unavoidably lead to grouse being disturbed a second time. In this situation one must withdraw from that part of the counting area completely and proceed to the opposite end of the area and begin counting on the other selected return route.

After each beat has been counted, the numbers of birds should be noted as: (1) number of coveys; (2) number of old birds; (3) number of young birds; (4) total number of birds; (5) ratio of young to old.

If it is found during counting on the selected routes of any area that, because of a build-up of birds ahead, the only alternative is to withdraw completely, the letter X should be placed against that area, denoting the fact that the counting of the beat was not completed.

After the second beat on each drive has been counted, the figures for both beats are added together and the total figure for that area is recorded along with the letter X, or two letters X if both beats were not completely counted.

This procedure is carried out on each and every drive. Any areas normally shot over outside the driving ground are counted by one beat only taken through the middle of that area and the figures recorded in the same way as for the drives.

Each keeper should count the sample areas on his own beat by himself and it is essential that he takes the same line through each area each year. The keeper doing the counting must never be tempted to hunt an extra part of any area or to take a zig-zag course if he is not seeing many birds. It is *essential* to be completely honest, otherwise a false total count may be submitted to the moor owner or shooting tenant which could be totally misleading and unfair to all concerned.

Counting begins on 20 July and is completed around 4 August. This period is chosen because by 20 July the coveys may be disturbed without harmful effect; and between 4 and 12 August the moor may be left quiet again before shooting commences.

Counting should never be attempted on a wet day or a day of high winds.

Counting should not be done in the evening after 5 p.m. because after that time of day it is harmful to disturb grouse from their territories.

The area which can be properly counted in each day is determined by the fitness of the dogs. Most keepers' dogs are exercised daily throughout the summer months, mainly in fields around the kennels, but this type of exercise, which is really all that a keeper can do with dogs at that time of year, is no preparation for hunting grouse on a heathery hillside. The dogs will become tired very quickly at the beginning of the counting programme, especially if the weather is warm, but will become very fit indeed within a few days of doing this type of work. Therefore, for the first day, a small area or drive should be selected and the size of the areas increased gradually as the dogs become hardened to the task. Eventually two areas can be counted with a break during the middle of the day.

During a spell of hot, dry weather, counting should be done in the early morning, never during the heat of the day.

When all the drives and other areas of the moor have been counted, the total number of birds for each area should be added together in each column of the counting sheet.

In our case, after many years of counting in this manner, we can, from these counts, assess to a fairly accurate degree how many grouse we should be able to shoot in the season ahead. We have found that if we count, say, *2000 individual grouse* at the end of July in the manner described, we should make a bag of *2000 brace* in the whole season.

We have found that the total season's bag has nearly always exceeded that of the predicted bag. We have also found that the greater the number of letters X in the count (denoting uncompleted counts), the greater the number of grouse killed in excess of the predicted bag.

This 'bag prediction' could also be called the surplus of grouse which may be culled for the season, but in some years it would be foolhardy to strive to achieve the predicted bag without considering other aspects of that particular season, i.e. condition of heather, condition of the birds, and the ratio of young to old birds (which can be worked out from the figures in the count). The counting system just described now plays a very important role in our management of grouse and has become an essential aid when planning shooting programmes.

The system works well but only if one is careful to carry out all the different aspects as described and never tempted to do something extra, or to be dishonest with oneself, which could lead to distorted figures. To do so would render the whole exercise worthless, with disastrous results.

The actual counting systems themselves should be capable of universal application on driving grouse moors of significant size throughout the country, but the interpretation of the figures obtained from the counting of the grouse must obviously depend, for any degree of reliability, on the relationship between the facts thus obtained and the actual experience of the bag obtained in each ensuing shooting season over a number of years. It is probable that there will be variation in this respect from moor to moor, but there is evidence to show that on other moors where our counting method has been tried the equation of 'grouse counted in July × 2 = bag obtainable for season' may be considered a reliable estimation if the sampling is properly carried out in the manner described. A variable factor, however, is the standard of shooting by the Guns. If in successive years the standard of shooting was markedly variable it would affect the relationship between grouse counted and grouse shot.

Appendix G

Sources of Information and Help

Alistair Aird, Logiealmond
Colin Adamson, Lauder
Elizabeth Bagshawe, Stamfordham
The Rt Hon the Lord Barnard, Raby Castle
Bill Brain, Garth Castle
Hugh Blakeney, Grantown-on-Spey
Sir John Brooke, Ardgay
Sir David Black, Elvendon Priory
Harry Beadle, Eggleston
The Rt Hon the Lord Biddulph, Makerston
Dick Burton, Brackenbank
Nicky Boulton, Farleyer
Anthony Briscoe, Barton Stacey
Daniel Carr, Whitchurch
James Copeland, Grantown-on-Spey
Chris Cornell, Staindrop
Ian Dickinson, Riding Mill
Peter Dickinson, Stocksfield
Robert Dickinson, Stocksfield
Archie Dykes, Logiealmond
Bill Drailsford, Lude
John Emmerson, Middleton-on-Tees
John Egle, Brackenbank
Sir Archibald Edmonstone, Duntreath Castle
Sepp Fawcett, Bollihope

Gough Thomas Garwood, Silverton
Rosemarie Gray, Eggleston
Dr Peter Hudson, Askrigg
Derek Harrison, Blanchland
Leslie Hogarth, Bollihope
Alan Ideson, Gunnerside
Shepard Johnson, Stoke-on-Trent
The Rt Hon the Lord Mansfield, Scone Palace
Duncan MacKinnon, Eggleston
The Hon G. E. I. Maitland Carew, Thirlstane Castle
Torquil McIntyre, Kinrara
Bill Makepiece, Middleton-on-Tees
Sandy McKenzie, Auchnafree
Nigel Pease, Bollihope
Simon Pease, Bollihope
The Rt Hon Earl Peel, Gunnerside
John Phillips, Lochwinnoch
Dr G. R. Potts, Fordingbridge
Gordon Roy, Glen Lyon
Neil Ramsay, Farleyer
Donald Renwick, Farleyer
William Redford, Tullybeagles
Robin Sandys-Clarke, Staindrop
Anthony Scott-Harden, Blanchland
Philip Scrope, Corbridge
Hugh Seccombe, Wonersh
Hamish Shaw, Ardgay
Neil Stanford, Chilmark
Robin Stormonth-Darling, Balvarran
Guy Severn, Streatley
Gilbert Smith, Brackenbank
Bettie Town, Blanchland
Alan Thornton, Witney
Miles Thimbleby, Whitchurch Canonicorum
Frank Usher, Dunglass
Dr Adam Watson, Banchory
Sir James Whitaker, Auchnafree
Kenneth Wilson, Leadhills

Charles Wyvill, Constable Burton
Lyndsay Waddell, Middleton-on-Tees
Richard Westmacot, Chathill
Jock Wilson, Abercairney
Mike Wolfe-Murray, Dirleton

Index